MICHAEL COLLINS
In His Own Words

MICHAEL COLLINS

In His Own Words

Edited by Francis Costello

GILL & MACMILLAN

Gill & Macmillan Ltd
Goldenbridge
Dublin 8
with associated companies throughout the world
© Francis Costello 1997
0 7171 2436 3

Index compiled by
Helen Litton

Design and print origination by
O'K Graphic Design, Dublin

Printed by
ColourBooks Ltd, Dublin

This book is typeset in 10/12 pt Plantin

A catalogue record for this book is available from the British Library.

3   5   4

To my father Frank Sr and my mother Kathleen, who prompted my interest in Michael Collins, and to their grandson Conor.

CONTENTS

PREFACE   ix

ACKNOWLEDGMENTS   xiii

CHRONOLOGY   xv

1. THE YOUNG MICHAEL COLLINS   1

2. COLLINS AT WAR: THE TRUCE   7

3. COLLINS THE MAN   32

4. COLLINS AND FINANCE   40

5. COLLINS: DEMOCRATIC POLITICS,
    PARTITION AND THE NORTH   55

6. COLLINS: THE TREATY, FREE STATE AND
    CIVIL WAR   66

7. COLLINS'S VISION FOR IRELAND   97

8. THE DEATH OF COLLINS   111

9. VINTAGE COLLINS   115

   NOTES   119

   BIBLIOGRAPHY   127

   INDEX   129

PREFACE

Michael Collins, Irish revolutionary *extraordinaire*, Anglo-Irish Treaty negotiator and founder of the independent Irish state, lived a total of thirty-one years, ten months and six days.

Like many leaders cut down early in life, his story has often been the stuff of myth, conjecture, and sometimes distortion. None of us has any way of knowing what Michael Collins would have accomplished had he lived. But we do know that his skills were still developing at the time of his death and his potential was great. Indeed, with the fullness of years his talents might well have transcended both Ireland and Anglo-Irish relations and attained a wider stage.

Clearly, Collins was more than a bit player in the passing parade, or another Irish patriot in the pantheon of Irish heroes, fighting gallantly against the odds before succumbing to superior force. It can be said that where he differs from other Irish patriots—none of whom lacked courage—was that perhaps more than many, Collins played to win. He had the vision, the tenacity, and at times the downright ruthlessness to create a new Ireland, and he had the fortitude to stand up for that vision whether his foe was the British Empire or in the end his former colleagues whom he saw as trying to thwart the democratic rights of the Irish people.

The Michael Collins revealed in these pages is no shrinking violet in whatever context he is seen to have operated: as Director of Intelligence for the IRA and its Director of Organisation, the Dáil Government's Minister for Finance, the head of the Irish Republican Brotherhood, as a leader of the Irish side in the 1921 Anglo-Irish negotiations, or as a principal architect of the fledgling independent Irish state in whose defence he died. And while he was far from a plaster saint, the sum total of Collins's contribution to Ireland shows that he was far more than the manager of an assassination squad, furtively manoeuvring the back alleys of Dublin on an old bicycle.

The intent of this effort is to allow Michael Collins to speak in his own unvarnished words, drawing from his letters, comments to colleagues, public statements, essays and other documents. The author is mindful of the concerns raised by Frank O'Connor many years ago on the challenge of offering a treatment of Michael Collins, especially where the subject's own words are concerned: 'What catches fire in speech rings cold in print; exaggeration, false emphasis, creeps in.' But in the absence of actual recordings of Collins's voice, it is in the written word that his essence remains. The silent film newsreel footage that exists along with collections of still photographs convey Collins in various poses, and sometimes in action. But we must look to what has survived of what he said and what he wrote for much of the substance of the man. It is this which helps to convey his tremendous organisational talent, as well as his cultural and economic vision for an independent Ireland.

While I have sought to provide the historical context to the often complex events about which Collins speaks herein, the objective has been to let readers form their own opinion of the man. At times what Collins says on a number of topics is, like many of his actions, contradictory. But this, I believe, underscores more than anything else the complexity of the man and why he continues as an enigma in many ways. At the same time, a careful reading of Collins's voice from various contexts and forums will hopefully serve to explain him better.

Can we in fact come to know the real Michael Collins through his own words? The reader will have to be the judge of that. What I have sought to do is give those seeking a deeper insight into an extraordinary young man, who shaped his times and his country as much as he was shaped by them, a platform from which to assess him.

Michael Collins has been dead for almost three-quarters of a century. He continues to be the subject of books, documentaries, plays and, more recently, a motion picture. His shadow continues to impose itself on the Irish scene and on many of the issues modern Ireland confronts. If his name is to be invoked in the current context, then surely we should know what it was he actually stood for and believed. In the process, perhaps we will also come to realise that Collins's life cannot be reduced to any single snapshot image.

Like other young leaders cut down in their prime, John F. Kennedy included, Michael Collins was still evolving.

Tragically, Ireland never came to witness what he could offer in a time of peace. As such, his potential for leadership was left unrealised. But his legacy remains rich and his story continues to both captivate and challenge Ireland.

It is hoped that this effort will provide a further portrait of Michael Collins and what he had come to represent during the final days of his young life. There was indeed the Michael Collins who was the soldier willing to die for Ireland—though preferably, he made clear, not as a martyr in another ill-planned protest, given his experience during the Easter Rising. But there was also Michael Collins the builder and the practical patriot. 'I am a war man in the day of war but I am a peace man in the day of peace,' he stated during the early days of the Irish Free State as he sought to build an independent Ireland while trying simultaneously to prevent a civil war which he knew would set Ireland back for years. That latter side of Collins— the nation builder—is one that must not be ignored if the meaning of his life is not to be devalued.

Herein Michael Collins is presented in all his phases: the lonely immigrant in London, the rebel leader on the run, the negotiator and would-be statesman, and also the visionary driven by a belief in what Ireland could be, but always willing at the same time to trust the democratic judgment of its people.

Michael Collins did not live to write his autobiography. The best we can do is attempt to let his voice speak to us in the context of his times.

ACKNOWLEDGMENTS

The effort contained in these pages is the distillation of many years spent quite unavoidably encountering Michael Collins in my research on the Irish Revolution and the development of an independent Ireland. The road to its completion has been greatly aided by many people of good will. I especially want to thank my wife Anne and our children for allowing me the time to undertake this project while also involving myself in other activities quite often at their expense.

Sincerest gratitude must also be rendered to Fergal Tobin, publisher, of Gill & Macmillan, for his kind help, good cheer and forbearance throughout all phases of my work on this project. There are legions of men and women in the various libraries, archives and public record offices to whom I am also indebted, including the staffs of the National Library of Ireland, the archival and manuscripts departments at Trinity College, University College, Dublin, Oxford University, the National Library of Wales, the House of Lords Records Office at Westminster and the Military History Bureau of the Irish Department of Defence, and Commandant Peter Young in particular. The men and women at the Public Records Office in Dublin—formerly the State Papers Office—also provided excellent assistance, as did their counterparts at the British Public Records Office at Kew.

I would also like to acknowledge Michael Farrell, John McColgan, Anne Rowland, Ray Dooley, John and Diddy Cullinane, Ita O'Connor and my late father-in-law James O'Connor, who helped and inspired me, each in their own way, during the various stages of this effort.

CHRONOLOGY

October 1890, Michael Collins is born near Clonakilty, Co. Cork.

1894, Collins enters Lisvaird National School.

1906, Collins emigrates to London at age 15 after passing entrance exam for British civil service, where from July 1906 to early 1910 he works as a clerk at the Post Office Savings Bank, followed by employment in private financial institutions.

November 1909, Collins is sworn in as a member of the Irish Republican Brotherhood.

1915, Collins joins Morgan Guaranty Bank's London office.

January 1916, Collins resigns position with Bank, returns to Ireland and joins the Irish Volunteers under command of Eoin McNeill.

April 1916, Collins participates in Easter Uprising as a combatant inside Dublin's GPO, and is afterwards transported to Frongoch prison camp, Wales, for internment.

December 1916, Collins is released under a general amnesty and returns to Ireland where he becomes a member of the IRB's Supreme Council.

February 1917, Collins becomes Secretary of the Irish National Aid Association to assist dependants of Irish political prisoners or those killed during the Easter Rising.

February 1918, Collins actively assists Éamon de Valera from England's Lincoln Jail.

May 1918, Britain undertakes 'German Plot' arrests, but Collins eludes British dragnet.

June 1918, British Government suppresses Sinn Féin, but movement wins second consecutive by-election for parliamentary seat with de Valera's victory in Co. Clare. Sinn

Féin's policy of abstentionism from House of Commons implemented.

1918–1919, Collins plays central role in setting up underground newspapers, building an intelligence network along with an arms smuggling system.

October 1918, British Government announces its intention of introducing conscription in Ireland.

December 1918, British General Election held with Sinn Féin winning vast majority of parliamentary constituencies, decimating the Irish Party in the process. Collins elected for Cork constituency.

January 1919, Dáil Éireann is established and Collins attends inaugural session at Dublin's Mansion House. Soon after he is named Minister of Finance for the Irish Republic. On same day, two policemen are killed in an ambush in County Tipperary by local Volunteers, setting the stage for the Anglo-Irish War.

November 1920, Guerilla war against British rule in Ireland escalates against backdrop of death via hunger strike of Cork's Lord Mayor Terence MacSwiney and the execution of Kevin Barry. 20 November is 'Bloody Sunday' when Collins's assassination squad wipes out British intelligence network in Dublin, an event which is followed by attack by British forces upon spectators at Croke Park.

December 1920, De Valera returns from almost two years spent in the US. Seeks truce with British, but Collins opposes effort.

January–June 1921, Guerilla war continues. Britain introduces curfews in key Irish population centres, along with heightening of martial law.

11 July 1921, Anglo-Irish Truce takes effect.

14 September 1921, Delegation to negotiate with British representatives appointed by Dáil Éireann.

10 October 1921, Irish delegation with Michael Collins meets Lloyd George for first time.

6 December 1921, Anglo-Irish Treaty Articles of Agreement signed.

January 1922, Treaty ratified by Dáil.

14 January 1922, Provisional Government appointed. Collins named as Chairman.

29 March 1922, Collins in London for conference.

13 April 1922, Four Courts occupied by Anti-Treatyite forces.

29 April 1922, Irish Conference to avert split ends in failure involving Collins, Griffith, de Valera and Brugha.

18 and 19 May 1922, Collins and de Valera meet in secret.

20 May 1922, Collins/de Valera pact announced.

27 May 1922, Collins meets with British officials in London after being summoned to explain pact with de Valera. He provides Draft Irish Constitution to British.

29 May 1922, British reject Draft Constitution.

1 June 1922, Lloyd George issues ultimatum to Free State Government calling for action against Anti-Treatyites.

5 June 1922, Joint Collins/de Valera appeal to support pact.

16 June 1922, Pact election held. Constitution published.

22 June 1922, Sir Henry Wilson assassinated in London.

26 June 1922, Winston Churchill issues ultimatum demanding that Free State attack Anti-Treatyites in Four Courts.

2 July 1922, Collins covertly sends Tom Cullen to London to plan escape for assassins of Henry Wilson. Effort is abandoned and the two men are subsequently executed by British.

12 July 1922, Provisional Government meets. Collins resigns as Chairman and becomes Commander-in-Chief of Army.

12 August 1922, Arthur Griffith dies.

18 August 1922, Collins is radioed terms of a ceasefire by Anti-Treatyite forces from Cork.

20 August 1922, Collins leaves Dublin ostensibly to conduct military tour of south-west Munster, first to Roscrea, then Limerick, Mallow and Cork.

21 August 1922, Collins tours Cork city and Macroom.

22 August 1922, 6:16 a.m. Collins leaves Cork city for Bandon, Clonakilty and Skibbereen via Macroom.

8 a.m. *En route* to Bandon via Macroom. Stops at Béal na Bláth for directions. Lunch in Clonakilty.

5 p.m. Leaves Skibbereen and heads for Bandon.

7.45 p.m. Collins is killed in ambush at Béal na Bláth.

1

THE YOUNG
MICHAEL COLLINS

Although he was not an Irish language enthusiast in the same mould as some of his contemporaries in the Irish independence effort, pride in things Irish, language, sports and music were part of his rich and complex persona. Throughout most of his life Collins preferred that his first name be written in the Irish spelling—Mícheál. He was of a clan that could trace itself back some four and a half centuries as chieftains in the Ó Coileáin tribe of Munster. And it was in the Irish form that his surname would appear on much of the written record, both official and clandestine in nature, that survives. An awareness of his Irishness and of his family's history filled Collins with a sense of pride and place throughout his life.

His rise to a leadership position in the Irish independence movement was acerbically described by his biographer Frank O'Connor as the efforts of a man who 'had made himself the leader of the whole revolutionary movement because he was up answering letters when everyone else was asleep'.[1]

It will be seen that Collins's dedication to detail and his capacity for work date back to his days as a schoolboy in west Cork, eager to learn and conscious of the world outside his native county.

He was born to humble beginnings, the youngest of eight. In early childhood Michael Collins developed a deep respect for older people. It was a sentiment probably heightened by the fact that his father was in his mid-60s when Collins was born. And so he meant it when in later years he said:

> I was a reverential kid. Reverence was not only instilled into me by my father; it seemed a natural trait. Great age held something for me that was awesome. I was much fonder of old people in the darkness than I was of young people in the daytime. It's at night you are able to get the value of old people. And it was listening to the old people that I got my ideas of nationality.[2]

Clearly Collins's attachment to older people began with his father—a man decades older than his mother. Although the elder Michael Collins died when his young son was 7, and was an aged man in all of young Michael's recollections of him, they formed a bond which Michael Collins would always value.

> All my early years I lived in childish wonder of my father. Although I was a lad of 7 when he died, he had already inspired me with the implicit faith in his goodness, his strength, his infallibility. I remember as it were yesterday an instance of my faith. . . . I was out in the fields with him one day, watching him at work, and I was on the turf below him. One of the stones, a good sized one, was dislodged at his feet and came rolling down straight at me. There was plenty of time for me to dodge it, but it never occurred to me to move. 'Twas my father's foot had done the business. Surely the stone could do me no harm. To this day I carry the mark in my instep where it crushed my foot.[3]

Although he would attend evening classes in accountancy and related subjects as an emigrant in London, Collins received the bulk of his formal education at the Clonakilty National School. It ended at the age of 15. What is striking is the apparent quality of that education in a relatively poor rural community. It was there that Collins was exposed to the classics, as well as Latin and Greek. And there he was inspired by a strongly pro-separatist view of Irish history conveyed to him by teachers who themselves had been previously educated in the hedge schools and were themselves disciples of Fenianism.

A unique glimpse of the early Collins, preparing to leave the safe haven of Clonakilty for life with his sister Hanna in London, is provided in a school composition he wrote titled 'Ancient and Modern Warfare'. It was written in 1906 when he was 15 years of age. The assignment was prepared for Mr Blewith's class in a school where the headmaster was Mr Crowley, a man for whom Collins was to hold a deep respect all his life. The essay portrays a boy with an awareness of the world and a dexterity with English vocabulary and composition that belied his years. It is also the work of a youth filled with promise, while at the same time revealing an attachment at an early age to matters involving war and warfare. But it is also filled with a sense of idealism tinged with the practical realities of the world he found himself living in as part of a small nation still under colonial rule. It was a balance he would later seek to alter.

The art of war is probably as old as the human race—certainly it is as old as human history. The remotest traditions show man making war upon his brother man even as the beasts of the field made war upon one another. It would seem as if nature aided and abetted this trend for the attainment of her inexorable ideal, the 'survival of the fittest'.

The world still contains a few surviving races and by going amongst them we can get a practical idea of what primitive warfare was like. . . . While, however, the mere mechanics of war have shown wonderful developments, the behaviour of the belligerents towards each other has not changed in any equivocal manner. War is more appallingly cruel and barbarous than ever. Of course it is also interspersed with mercy, as was shown by the efforts of Napoleon's soldiers to save from drowning the Russian soldiers under whom they had broken the ice with their cannons. It will be contended that the enemies' wounds are cared for . . . that the Red Cross is conspicuous on every battlefield, but the main thing is that the battlefield remains and besides, the instruments of warfare are deadlier and the number often disabled tremendously large.

The argument that war has become less revolting or less ugly is futile. The plain truth is that it has become more terrible but with this we may see some hope. At the present time England and

Germany are having a ludicrous but not inexpensive race for armaments. England is trying to bully Germany into ceasing to build dreadnoughts, Germany replying by rattling the sword in the scabbard. Mutual fear of annihilation combined with the awful destruction which would ensue prevent them from going to war. This development then is the hope and may lead to the realisation of Tennyson's dream about the 'Parliament of Man, the Federation of the World'.[4]

Reading this essay almost a century after it was written, one is struck by how Collins's later proposal, expressed during the 1921 Anglo-Irish negotiations for transforming the British Commonwealth into a World Federation linking the nations of the world in a system that would preserve world peace and in which Ireland could take its place, took root as a schoolboy in Clonakilty. Indeed, we see at this early stage of development an inclination towards pacifism. Later his ideas would meet with minimal success in the corridors of Downing Street from people supposedly more skilled in the ways of international politics than he. But from the standpoint of later efforts at international organisation, we see that Collins's ideas were indeed visionary.

His emigration to London in July 1906—four months before his sixteenth birthday—would mark the beginning of eight years spent away from Ireland. Before he left home, he successfully sat for the British Civil Service exam. He had already learned how to type before he emigrated. Like many other young Irishmen, the civil service became the entry point to his first job in London—a junior clerkship in the post office in west Kensington. The job paid £70 per year. The restless youth resigned, however, after two years, stating that he discovered 'I was in a blind alley in the civil service.' Collins describes what followed:

> . . . several years of other jobs, none of which satisfied my ideas of opportunity. First I took a minor post in a stockbroker's office, then a clerkship in the Guarantee Trust Company of New York at its branch in the City [London]. But with each passing year I felt more and more convinced that London for me held as little real opportunity as did Ireland.[5]

4

But it is during this time that Collins's sense of what he termed 'real opportunity' grew to encompass more than his own personal advancement. He became a member of the Irish Republican Brotherhood in 1909 and, like the rest of its members, sworn to take the steps necessary to achieve an independent Ireland by any means necessary, came to adopt a political agenda still far outside the mainstream of Irish nationalism. He had left Ireland for London, but the Irish nationalism of the separatist variety that had been drilled into him by his teachers had not. He had clearly made a decision somewhere during his early years in London that took him away from the ideals of pacifism expressed in his essay to the underground world of secret societies and the hatching of a violent revolt against British rule in Ireland. On 25 April 1914 he would reach another milestone when he enrolled as a member of the Irish Volunteers in London. Soon afterwards he took possession of his first rifle and started drilling in a gymnasium in King's Cross.

In the next two passages we see how Collins had come to view himself and the skills he possessed as he stood on the threshold of the most dramatic change in his life to date.

However happy I happen to be in a particular job, the thought is always with me that my future is otherwise than among the facts and figures of money. Yet I do not really dream of greater things . . . only the thought is always there.[6]

The trade I know best is the financial trade, but from study and observation I have acquired a wide knowledge of social and economic conditions and have specially studied the building trade and unskilled labour. Proficient in typewriting, but have never been tested for speed. Thorough knowledge of double entry system and well used to making balances and balance sheets.[7]

In London, his time outside of work largely saw him involved in Irish cultural and sporting activities with other Irish emigrants. He also enjoyed regular visits to the theatre and pursued further education in the evening. In short order he became both treasurer of the IRB cell in London, as well as the treasurer for that city's chapter of the Gaelic Athletic Association (GAA).

At the end of 1915, two things had become clear to Collins. Whatever hope constitutional nationalism held of gaining Home Rule for Ireland had been dashed on the rocks by British double dealing and its outright surrender to the unionists of the North. On a personal basis, like many other young Irishmen living in England at that time, he had no desire to be conscripted into the British ranks for action in Europe. He would use his experience with a weapon against British rule, not to enhance it. He went to Dublin briefly, but was directed back to London by Tom Clarke and Seán Mac Diarmada—his superiors in the IRB. Collins's stay in the British capital would be shorter this time, however. On 16 January 1916 Conscription became law. Michael Collins was already on a boat bound for Dublin and insurrection. The ex-British postal clerk had now embarked on a journey that, within a few years, would soon make him the most wanted man in the British Empire.

2

COLLINS AT WAR: THE TRUCE

O nce in Dublin Collins, the would-be revolutionary, bided his time. He found work with Count Plunkett, whose son was soon to meet a tragic death before a British firing squad. The young Corkman described his 'temporary employment' in a letter to his sister Hannie in London.

> I'm still in Dublin doing a very little bit. Working three days a week 10 to 4 as financial adviser to Count Plunkett for which I get lunch and £1 a week . . . This place has many advantages over London in spite of everything. It's just lovely to see the mountains of a morning. My present job is at Kimmage far out— seems to be as remote as Woodfield but it's only a short walk and a penny tram ride from the Emerald pasture at College Green.[1]

His career change became complete during the following two months. A Dublin firm of chartered accountants that had next employed him in a temporary capacity noted that after it had sent him to County Wexford 'on a liquidation matter . . . we never saw or heard from him after Easter Week'.[2] The company was not left totally in the lurch, however, since Collins only collected one week of the month's pay he had earned.

On Easter Monday, 24 April 1916, Michael Collins reported for his last assignment at a post office. But this time it was of a different type and one on his own terms. Still wearing ordinary clothing, Collins was at first intercepted by an Irish Volunteer sentry near Nelson's Pillar. The would-be revolutionary approached O'Connell Street on a bicycle, a rifle draped across the back of it. When asked his business, Collins nodded forward in the direction of the GPO and remounted his bicycle and nonchalantly cycled away. One week later the Volunteer would notice Collins among the ranks of the prisoners, with him being led down O'Connell Street, with the GPO and much of the centre of the city in ruins. This time Collins, covered in dust, was wearing the uniform of an officer in the Volunteers.

It was a spectacle that Collins had no desire to see repeated. Although proud of his participation within the nerve centre of the GPO, as an officer under Joseph Plunkett, his practical mind saw a better way of waging war against the British Empire. Collins's criticism afterwards of leaders of the Rising was as blunt and to the point as that ever offered by any insider:

It is so easy to fault the actions of others when their particular actions have resulted in defeat. . . . I admired the men in the ranks and the womenfolk thus engaged. But at the same time . . . the actions of the leaders should not pass without comment. They have died nobly at the hands of the firing squads. So much I grant. But I do not think the Rising week was an appropriate time for the issue of a [memorandum] couched in poetic phrases, nor of actions worked out in similar fashion. Looking at it from the inside . . . it had the air of a Greek tragedy about it. . . . Of Pearse and Connolly, I admire the latter the most. Connolly was a realist. Pearse the direct opposite . . . There was an air of earthy directness about Connolly. I would have followed him through hell . . . But honestly I doubt very much if I would have followed Pearse—not without some thought anyway. I think chiefly of Tom Clarke and Mac Diarmada. Both built on the best foundations. Ireland will not see another Seán Mac Diarmada. These are sharp reflections. On the whole I think the Rising was bungled terribly, costing many a good life. It seemed at first to be well organised, but afterwards became subjected to panic decisions and a great lack of very essential organisation and cooperation.[3]

Indeed, from then on Collins would strive to heed the advice given by Seán Mac Diarmada: 'Never allow yourselves to be cooped up inside the walls of a building again.'[4] As Collins stood outside the GPO waiting to be marched away to an unknown fate, he watched quietly the scene of surrender and humiliation before him. His mind made a snapshot of the name and face of the British officer who stripped Tom Clarke naked —the oldest of the rebel leaders—in front of them. The gentleman would be hearing from Collins on another occasion.

If Frongoch was indeed a 'University of Revolution', then Michael Collins must be seen as one of its famous graduates. For it was during his eight months in confinement there that he honed his skills as a guerrilla tactician and as a leader of men, and where, most important, he would forge friendships that would enable him to set in place organisations both civil and military that would rock British rule in Ireland in a way it had never been challenged before.

At Frongoch, one fellow internee who shared a hut with Collins recalled that he 'was dressed in very good clothes, but wore no collar or tie, and his boots were army boots, unpolished'.[5] But Collins was at the same time among the most boisterous of the internees at Frongoch's hut-formationed North Camp. He led the way with wrestling, pillow fights and other expressions of his boundless energy. But overall his time there was spent in earnest. It was there that the IRB was reborn and Collins was at the heart of that rebirth. The execution of Mac Diarmada and Clarke, among other IRB men from the secret society's leadership who took part in the Rising, created a vacancy at the top that Collins proved only too willing to fill.

Upon his release from Frongoch in December 1916 under an amnesty granted by the same British prime minister he would confront across the Cabinet table at Downing Street five years later—David Lloyd George—Collins threw himself into the work of prison relief, becoming head of the Prisoners and Dependants Association. In that role he tied the newly released prisoners to the association and with them created the necessary cover for re-establishing the Volunteer organisation. But beyond the enormous range of official responsibilities Collins held, there was also strong evidence of his personal devotion to those still in prison that went beyond his role with the Prisoners and Dependants Association. Compelling evidence of the dedication he attached to his duties is evidenced ironically in his correspondence to Austin Stack who was destined to become his enemy.[6]

Collins's first foray into the structures of a political movement came in October 1917 when he was narrowly elected to the executive of the Sinn Féin organisation, with de Valera replacing Arthur Griffith as the movement's president.

In the following letter of 9 June 1918 we see Collins's willingness to share with Stack one of his most precious worldly possessions—his books. The book list offered Stack is also useful in painting a picture of Collins's diverse reading interests, an avocation he appears to still maintain at this time despite the intense pressures now upon him.

The following books I have which may be of some interest to you. All Duffy's Library of Ireland 22 volumes. Tone, old edition. Jail Journal. Lost Conquest. Apology. John Mitchell. Burke on Fronde. Hegarty, Young Ireland. Casement. Travel. Mangan. Essays. Complete Poems. Life and Writings. Barrington's Rise and Fall . . . Bulfin's Rambles in Erin. Myles Byrne, Notes on An Irish Exile. Art McMurrough. Volunteers of 1782. Barry O'Brien's Life of Parnell and One Hundred Years of Irish History. Speeches from the Dock. Numerous volumes of poetry such as Irish ballads, Rising of the Moon, etc. Spirit of the Nation, Songs of Freedom. New Irish Song Book. Songs of the Gael. Many Irish textbooks, Robinson Crusoe in Irish among them, all good works.[7]

Maintaining discipline within the ranks of the Irish Volunteers was one of the key challenges occupying Collins for much of 1918. This directive to the brigade commandant of the mid-Limerick Brigade is illustrative of what he confronted.

It was not until this moment that de V [de Valera] gave me D. Hannigan's dispatch with your note attached. The course of a particular coy [company] or battalion detaching itself from its own local headquarters is most irregular.

You might get all the local details from Con [Collins]. The matter is coming up at the next meeting of the staff. It's unlikely that the Ballylanders crowd will be allowed to do as they like. A brigade election was held in that area (east Limerick) recently and all parties agreed to abide by the decision [for] two months [from about 1 May] at the end of which a new election will be held.[8]

Questions about how best to raise in public via the press the matter of prisoners' rights were also discussed in Collins's correspondence with Stack, who had led a prisoners' strike over the conditions in Belfast Jail. A letter of 27 June 1918 indicates how much Collins, a non-lawyer, had come to grasp some of the complexities of the legal questions at hand. The letter begins on a light note, with Collins expressing to Stack his hope that 'the Afton medium [cigarettes] was right. You do allow yourself tobacco, I understood. If not I'm sorry.'

What I'd like to have is your opinion on this. You will probably know that the King has made an affidavit with regards to the things that happened in Belfast and the treatment meted out to the prisoners. It is suggested that it would be worthwhile for the sake of publicity to issue one against the governor of the jail. Then apply for an injunction on the grounds of urgency, to have the case heard during the vacation. Counsel would be required but it is hinted that Healy would do the job practically free. If the injunction [was] granted there would very likely be an application by the Crown for change of venue. There would in that event be further battle between the lawyers. The idea is that on some one of these occasions the affidavit would be read and might get into the papers. Do you think it is worthwhile?

There are several things to be considered. It would be recognising jurisdiction. The venue might be changed (even if the injunction were given) and it would be useless going on in Belfast. Of course, before that sufficient publicity might have been achieved. Anyway, will you please send out as soon as you can a complete version of what happened like your Mountjoy document . . . I am sorry we had not a proper realisation of the situation that existed at the time of the trouble in Belfast. An attempt ought I think be made to inform us if there is a sort of repetition. There is only one thing we can do now and we'll concentrate on that in case of a recurrence. There are other things I'd like to tell you but they cannot be put into writing.[9]

On the personal side, Collins's feelings for his comrades in prison and his desire to help them further is conveyed in this letter to Stack of 11 February 1919.

> My kindest regards to Fin [Fionan Lynch] as well as the others. Even if I don't always mention them, I never forget them, nor what you're going through . . . All your remembrances will be conveyed faithfully. I will stick a note in the papers to reassure the prisoners' friends.[10]

A few months later Collins informed Stack that he was 'attending to the clothes. Jim will have them tomorrow. I got the bill too, but I don't like presenting it to Jim. May I pay it?'[11] He expressed similar sentiments once to Stack on 12 September 1919—in a letter in which it was obvious that Collins's own family members were visiting the prisoner.

> Glad to hear you are fixed all right for tobacco and such. You need have no qualms about any trouble any of my family are put to. It's really no trouble for them and I feel it a sort of way of paying back debts so many families have troubled on my account because of the other member of my family—if you get what I mean. My sister is not so young. So you needn't be afraid on that point either. She is eleven years older than I am and twice that much wiser.[12]

In the same letter Collins expressed his opinion to Stack of the latter's desire to take an opening on the Kerry Council and on the efforts of those who wanted Stack to make Tralee his base of operations after his release: 'My own idea would be that you'd be indispensable in Dublin and I don't think any consideration would change my mind in that regard.'[13] But in the end Stack's future would be largely in Dublin where he would serve in the Dáil Cabinet, with Collins as Minister of Home Affairs. Ironically, it was in that post that his personal animosity with Collins developed after Collins, during a Cabinet meeting in 1920, referred bluntly to the manner in which Stack administered his department as a 'bloody joke'.

Although he was now also involved in what were the rudiments of Sinn Féin as a political organisation, Collins's correspondence with Stack indicates a certain discomfort by the summer of 1918 in the way those with a political bent in the

Irish separatist movement were behaving. Clearly Collins is also suffering from a certain despondence with the circumstances in which he finds himself.

There is one thing about loneliness—it gives one a feeling of independence. I am bad company at present anyway. . . . Things are happening in Sinn Féin circles that are somewhat calculated to upset one. Certain well-known personages in the movement, officers in fact, have been hob-nobbing with people like James O'Connor [British MP]. The Ard Comhairle is tomorrow and I shall give you an account of it. There are certain resolutions being proposed with a view to unearth and destroy any attempt at compromise. The Sinn Féin organisation lacks direction at the present moment. The men who ought to be directing things are too lax and spend little or no time at No. 6. Unfortunately I cannot go into details—and in any case we'll probably stop the negotiating. In the meantime I am giving you a tip that all is not as well as it might be. As a result of the interview I am having tomorrow I may have something important to communicate about conscription. Would like to have your opinion about the advisability of holding I.V. [Irish Volunteers] convention this year. In the ordinary way it is due end of October. The conscription business may intervene, but even if it doesn't, I don't think we ought to have such an assembly for a variety of reasons.[14]

The results of the 1918 General Election, as well as Sinn Féin's own subsequent efforts, helped the movement emerge into a pro-separatist umbrella organisation that encompassed a wide range of interests favouring Irish independence. But it was still not a state of affairs with which Collins was entirely comfortable. He was afraid that the national movement he was trying to reinvigorate would be taken over by the self-serving. By now (the end of 1918) Collins had both feet firmly planted in both sides of the Irish independence movement—the physical force side via the IRB and the reconstituted Irish Volunteers on one side, and as a member of the Sinn Féin executive on the other. With the establishment of Dáil Éireann as the Alternative Government for Ireland by Sinn Féin in January 1919, he would serve as Minister for Finance for the

Irish Republic as well as an elected member of the Dáil itself for his native Cork.

But as 1918 drew to a close, it wasn't politics but the revitalisation of the physical force movement that was foremost on Collins's mind. His correspondence to Stack of 18 November 1918—coinciding with Sinn Féin's overwhelming display of electoral strength—shows how pivotal a role he was by then playing in the creation of command and divisional structures for the Irish Volunteers. Based on the work he had done up to this point, it is clear that south-west Munster was being singled out as the strongest area for a return to arms. It is also clear from his communication that Collins was already by then warming to the hat he would wear as the Director of Intelligence for the Volunteers by noting the movements of British soldiers and policemen injured in confrontations with Sinn Féin supporters.

As a result of various encounters, there were 125 cases of wounded soldiers treated at the Dublin hospitals last night. . . . A policeman too was in a very precarious condition up to a few days ago when I ceased to take any further interest in him. He was unlikely to recover.

I have been trying to think out what the arrangements for divisional groupings ought to be. I am inclined to think that a divisional officer with his staff must be concentrated on a given locality and that they must be appointed by H.Q. Such divisions will be necessary in a short time in Cork, Kerry, Limerick, Tipperary, Clare, and other places probably.

We are having a good deal of trouble with Clare. We'll likely work it out harmoniously in the end. That matter arose on our suggestion of division of the Clare Brigade into three. At first Brennan [Frank Brennan] was taking it all right, and in fact Dick Mulcahy and I had agreed with him on the actual areas, but in the course of a few days afterwards, when we met him with some of his brigade commanders, he and Hunt wanted to tout a divisional staff before any such division of brigade was carried through. Now I believe Brennan has the hell of a grievance against me, but that won't make me expire [sic]. He has resigned from the executive too.[15]

14

Remarkably, despite all of these pressures and sources of difficulty described herein, Michael Collins also made a point of monitoring international developments, especially in relation to the likelihood of an armistice in Europe. He also followed developments in Russia where Allied forces seemed poised to attack Russia in an attempt to topple the fledgling Bolshevik regime. In his correspondence with Stack, Collins also emphasised the relevance between such developments and a return to violence by the Volunteers in Ireland.

> Take Bulgaria, for instance. I think the Bolshevik idea is the force there. Time will tell. The only thing that concerns us in this country and even if nothing comes [is how] we can go into the wilderness again and maybe better be prepared for the next clash . . . I wish to God there was more of the people out whom we could discuss things with and in whom confidence could be reposed.[16]

On 11 November 1918 Europe again loomed large in Collins's attention.

> The *Manchester Guardian* says the generals may make an armistice 'but who can make peace' in an article on Saturday last. The whole article is an apologia for Austria-Hungary and the above remark comes into an article bewailing the disintegration of what they used to call the Hamshackle Empire. 'The Allies', it says, 'cannot walk through a country where all the conditions of Bolshevism are being rapidly reproduced.' The underworld is arising and I for one am far more hopeful than I ever was. The position is changing so rapidly that it would be hazardous to make any shots at what the future is likely to bring forth. It does, however, look as if the Austrian surrender and proposal for armistice come from the reprise of the privileged classes and that the soldiers who represent the masses are fighting on. Therefore, an armistice will give the Allies no power over the area any more than the armistice with Bulgaria did over that country . . . The surrender of Turkey and the opening of the Dardanelles is designed wholly I think . . . for an attack on the Russian Bolsheviks. Movement interesting altogether. Will communicate further with you on this peace subject as it is a matter that is of vital importance to us.[17]

Two events transpired on 21 January 1919 which covered Collins's dual interest in the Sinn Féin movement and physical force. They were also apocryphal from the standpoint of Ireland's prospects as an independent nation. On the same day that Dáil Éireann met in its inaugural session at Soloheadbeg, Co. Tipperary, an Irish Volunteer unit under Dan Breen and Sean Treacy, acting independently of Volunteer headquarters, shot dead two RIC members in a roadside confrontation. It marked the opening act of the War of Independence.

Unlike others in the newly formed Dáil Cabinet—including Éamon de Valera—Collins was not repulsed by Treacy and Breen's unauthorised act of violence. It created the situation Collins wanted, whereby the physical men in the independence movement could now assert themselves over the more politically minded and provide the opportunity for a violent revolution. In view of the failure of Sinn Féin's representatives to win a hearing at the Paris Peace Conference for Ireland's right to self-determination or even a general acknowledgment of that right from US President Woodrow Wilson, the resort to violence became necessary to Collins. In short order as Adjutant General and Director of Organisation for the Volunteers—the name IRA came later—Collins became the only member of the general headquarters staff to have the authority to approve attacks on RIC barracks in independent operations around Ireland.

Collins, however, continued well into May 1919 to express his concern that too many in the Sinn Féin leadership were lagging behind in their support for the physical force side of the independence effort. He also expressed his frustrations in a letter to Stack on 17 May about the manner in which he felt loose talk in Dáil Éireann was responsible for revealing information to the enemy, e.g. that Harry Boland was in America.

The position is intolerable. The policy now seems to be to squeeze out anyone who is tainted with strong fighting ideas . . . Of course many of the Dáil Ministers are not eligible for the Standing Committee and only one-third of the entire number may be members of the Dáil. The result is that there is a Standing Committee of malcontents and their first act is to appoint a pacifist secretary and to announce the absence of Harry Boland.

Our own people give away in a moment what the Detective Division has been unable to find out in five weeks . . . If this reaches you, you will I hope give an account of the position, conditions, surveillances, etc.

One day later Collins elaborated further to Stack about his frustrations and also offered his assessment of the inevitable fracturing he saw in all revolutionary movements.

It seems to me that official Sinn Féin is inclined to be ever less militant and ever more political, theoretical . . . There is I suppose the effect of the tendency of all revolutions moving to divide themselves into component parts. Now the moral force department have been probably affected by British propaganda. . . . You can see it at work. In the minds of the moderates it climbs to the surface in all sorts of rumours, whispers, suggestions of differences between certain people—all that sort of thing. It's rather pitiful and at times somewhat disheartening. At the moment, I'm awfully fed up.[18]

The extent to which Collins had by now become so immersed in almost every facet of the Irish Revolution, including the structure of local brigades and the need to develop an efficient system for receiving reports at general headquarters in Dublin of their activities, is shown by a correspondence of 8 August 1919 to Frank Barrett, Commandant of the mid-Clare Brigade. It was signed by Collins in his role as Adjutant General.

The following man is to transfer to your area: Sean O'Grady, Cappamore, Crusheen. He was formerly Battalion Commandant in the Meath Brigade. Please have him connected up. . . . Up to the time of writing the report form covering the activities of your brigade for the month of July has not come to hand, neither in fact has the form for June. For some reason, I omitted to remind you of this latter omission already.[19]

One brigade commandant describes Collins's directness in evaluating a man's performance during a request in person for more weapons.

17

Not bad. See here, if I had a few more brigades of the quality of yours I'd be happy. Luckily the good ones outnumber the bad by a fair majority. Would it surprise you to know there's never a damned shot fired except at a bird . . . Well, it's a fact.[20]

But one problem that refused to go away for him was an even more vexing one: how to deal with the twin problems of a chronic lack of arms and ammunition. The following communication to an IRA brigade commandant on 6 October 1919 offers both sympathy and a candid statement of the situation.

The question of armament and of course ammunition for same is a chancy business. Captured equipment of this kind is a mere one thousandth of what we really need. Purchase of arms is difficult and also dangerous to those engaged in this vital task. I will worry them all I possibly can, but at the moment your allocation must remain as it is.[21]

But for those who did little with arms and ammunition they had been allocated, Collins had a different type of message on 17 May 1919:

When you ask me for ammunition for guns which have never fired a shot in this fight, my answer is a simple one. Fire shots at some useful target or get to hell out of it.[22]

In matters involving the carrying out of orders as well as the efficient use of all weapons, Collins was equally candid about the importance of accountability in the chain of command.

I take it as said. No need to apportion out the blame. It was badly organised and could be faulted in a dozen ways. Therefore:
1. You, the Brigade Commander, are responsible for the failure.
2. As much discredit should be lavished on your I.O. [Intelligence Officer].
3. The raising party commandant was at fault in not withdrawing his men at once when the situation was a hopeless one.
    See that it does not happen again.[23]

As Minister for Finance, as we will see, Collins worked hard to assure accountability in public expenditures. But he also, quite remarkably, found the time throughout the War of Independence to ensure that those at the brigade level, given copies of the IRA propaganda organ *An t-Oglach*, forwarded payment in a timely fashion.

> Sixteen shillings and eight not to hand, after numerous requests. A small sum of money—agreed. Yet multiply this trivial amount by say, one hundred—what have you? A largish sum. I do not request, I insist.[24]

But the same Collins who was so laden down with such roles as IRA Adjutant General and the organisation's Director of Intelligence—in addition to serving as the Dáil Government's Minister for Finance—also internalised the sufferings of IRA men in prison, especially those who faced death. He became fixated on plans to get the men out of prison by any means necessary. When he paced the floor and waited impatiently for a report as to whether or not an attempt had been successful, we see Collins at his most loyal and also his agonised condition. The scheduled hanging of Kevin Barry on 1 November 1920 got his attention particularly. Collins proposed that a wall of the prison be blown away and his men would then fight their way to where Barry was and save him from the hangman. The plan failed. When the men got to Mountjoy Jail the streets were surrounded by throngs of women praying for Barry's life and soon his soul, making the break-in attempt impossible. Collins, soon after the sad news reached him, entered a room at Devlin's bar looking forlorn. 'The poor kid', he muttered under his breath.[25]

In the case of those on hunger strike, while he did not support this form of protest, he stood faithfully by the protesters. Such was the case with Terence MacSwiney and the eleven other IRA prisoners who joined his hunger strike. An effort on Collins's part, along with the Lord Mayor's wife, to persuade MacSwiney to end his protest failed. He then attempted other means for getting MacSwiney out of Brixton Prison alive. On 26 August 1921, in a cryptic communication to Art O'Brien in London, three weeks into the Lord Mayor's protest, Collins wrote:

As already indicated to you three have gone across last night and the others went this morning. You will get our people together, that is to say, yourself and mobilise every possible bit of assistance that can be secured in London. One man who accompanied the Corkmen is already known to you, and to _____. He will be their guide.[26]

But as time went by and MacSwiney's condition became more frail, the plans for an escape were set aside. Perturbed by an attempt by someone in MacSwiney's party of relatives in London to terminate the medical attention given him, Collins issued this instruction to Art O'Brien:

I may say that it was very wrong of anybody to suggest the discontinuance of medical treatment . . . The view is that medical treatment should be availed of . . . We would rely on the etiquette of the profession in so far as the administering of nutriment is concerned.[27]

Conscious of the need to preserve MacSwiney's strength, Collins also advised O'Brien to curtail his scheduled visits to him, 'so long as we are kept informed'. He also expressed his awe of MacSwiney and the other inmates in Cork in two consecutive letters to O'Brien on 25 and 28 September.

[MacSwiney's] prolongation of life seems to be absolutely wonderful—in fact little short of miraculous. The miraculous thing is that not one of the whole crowd had any organic defect. This is more remarkable in Terry's case than in the others as he had such a trying time for the past four years and a half.[28]

After MacSwiney's death on 25 October 1920, Collins and Arthur Griffith immediately ordered the remaining IRA prisoners still alive in Cork Jail to end their protest. It was to mark the last IRA hunger strike of the War of Independence. Collins clearly had other notions in the months to follow as to how best to hit at the British Empire.

For the twelve assassinations and several woundings carried out by the IRA against the British intelligence agents on Bloody Sunday, Collins offered no remorse. To him they constituted 'legitimate acts of self-defence forced upon us by English oppression'. He was equally blunt about why the men were chosen as targets, as well as the means employed:

> Let it be remembered that we did not initiate the war, nor were we allowed to choose the lines along which the war developed . . . Our only way to carry on the fight was by organised and bold guerrilla warfare. But this in itself was not enough. However successful our efforts, however many 'murders' we committed—England could always reinforce her army. She could always replace every soldier she lost . . . To paralyse the British machine it was necessary to strike at individuals outside the ranks of the military. Without her Secret Service working at the top of its efficiency England was helpless . . . robbed of the network of this organisation throughout the country, it would be impossible to find 'wanted' men. Without their criminal agents in the capital it would be hopeless to effect the removal of those leaders marked down for murder. It was these men we had to put out of the way.[29]

It was also Collins's candid assessment that 'spies are not ready to step into the shoes of their departed confederates as are soldiers to fill up the front line in honourable battle' [ibid.] But as confident as he was in his public defence of the actions taken on Bloody Sunday, there was an at least tacit admission of over-zealousness to Richard Mulcahy afterwards regarding the killing in cold blood of British ex-Captain Patrick McCormack on that day. Collins's comments also make it clear that a number of the British servicemen and ex-servicemen killed had not in fact been members of the British Secret Service as claimed. Collins advised Mulcahy as to the best way to respond to a letter from the dead man's mother. Attention might be brought to the way in which Collins clinically describes the assassinations as 'cases' as though he were an insurance claims adjuster evaluating an applicant. The manner in which Collins attempts to deflect the selection of McCormack and the other non-British intelligence officers away from his chosen 'squad' and place the responsibility on to the shoulders of the Dublin Brigade is also noteworthy. That Collins and Mulachy were communicating more than a year after the incident and during a time when they were attempting to establish the Free State Government as provided under the

1921 Anglo-Irish Treaty and were by then actually in need of British cooperation, may also have been a factor behind Collins's conciliatory tone.

> With reference to the case, you will remember that I stated on a former occasion that he was a Secret Service agent. You will also remember that several of the names of the November cases were just regular officers. Some of the names were put on by the Dublin Brigade. So far as I remember McCormack's name was one of these . . . In my opinion, it would be as well to tell Mrs McCormack that there was no particular case against her son, but just that he was an enemy soldier.[30]

Aside from the incidents of Bloody Sunday, which also included a deadly attack on spectators and players at a Gaelic football match at Dublin's Croke Park by members of the British military and the RIC, the period encompassing October to December 1920 marked some of the bloodiest fighting and provocative occurrences in the conflict. At the end of October Terence MacSwiney, the Lord Mayor of Cork, died after a 74 day hunger strike as a political prisoner. One week later, despite a public outcry and protestations from the Catholic clergy, 18-year-old IRA member Kevin Barry was hanged at Mountjoy Jail. Soon afterwards the IRA responded with a series of attacks against British military convoys and barracks, the most deadly of which occurred at Kilmichael in west Cork. The British Government, in turn, imposed martial law upon Ireland's south-western counties, while also enforcing a vigorous curfew on the streets of Dublin.

The end of that year also gave rise to a number of peace initiatives. One undertaking involved Fr Michael O'Flanagan, a moderating force in Sinn Féin. At the same time Archbishop Patrick Clune of Australia, with the apparent encouragement of Lloyd George, came to Dublin on a peace mission and met with Michael Collins and Arthur Griffith. The following month, Éamon de Valera, recently returned from a stay of eighteen months in the United States, called for an 'easing off' by the IRA of its attacks on British forces. His call was rejected by the Dáil and the IRA, with Michael Collins helping lead the opposition in January after sensing that too overt a display of a desire for peace on the part of Sinn Féin would lead to the weakest of terms from the British. Galway County Council's call upon Dáil Éireann to seek a truce also met with his ire, given that this was a county which he felt had not pulled its weight thus far in the conflict in comparison with other sections of the country.

> A truce would have been obtained after the burning of Cork by the forces of the Crown in December 1920, had our leaders acted with discretion. There is every reason to believe that the British Government was minded to respond favourably to the endeavours of Archbishop Clune . . . but the English attitude hardened through the precipitate actions of certain of our public men and public bodies. . . . Several of our most important public men gave evidence of an over-keen desire for peace, while proposals were being made and considered. So it was that, although terms of the truce had been virtually agreed upon, the British statesmen abruptly terminated the negotiations when they discovered what they took to be signs of weakness in our council.[31]

Instead of peace there would be more war. It was a decision that Collins helped force as much as any leader in the Dáil or the IRA. But with the decision came a desire on the part of Collins and Mulcahy to make necessary changes in the IRA's mode of operations, especially as the British forces throughout the spring of 1921 deployed their forces more effectively and in fact implemented a flying-column approach of their own. The imposition of martial law and curfews also led to the increased arrest of both IRA members and their officers. On 26 March 1921 Collins, by then the IRA's Director of Organisation, responded to a proposal authored by Mulcahy for the more efficient deployment of men and munitions around the country. At the core of Mulcahy's proposal was a numbering system for mapping the strength of the IRA divisions.

> It might be possible to combine numbers 2 and 3 [Tyrone, Armagh, Derry and Down] but the Adjutant would have tremendous responsibility in the way of organising and regrouping. The same applies to numbers 4 and 5 [the Midlands] but if we can get suitable direction from the Director for Training, it would be more important . . . to establish the engineering arm

23

first . . . all these instructions will have to come up a good deal at tomorrow's meeting.[32]

Central to Collins's actions and the decisions he made on virtually every front was his use of intelligence gathering. He sought to beat the British by outwitting them at their own game: infiltrating them with spies. His army of spies ran the gamut, from hotel porters to domestic servants to trusted members of the RIC's Detective Branch, to within the British Administration at Dublin Castle itself. The following secret correspondence to William O'Brien, the President of the Irish Congress of Trade Unions, on 9 July 1921, is valuable for underscoring Collins's appreciation of the role Irish labour had played in the Irish Revolution and also of the depth of the information he was able to obtain on Britain's movements in Ireland on the espionage front headlined 'Enemy Spies in Ireland'. Collins's communication to O'Brien stated:

I got the following from a very reliable source: 'Dublin Castle is selecting men from the military there to go around the country anywhere there is a trade union of any description to pose as coming from the executive of the particular union. Men so selected are to be supplied with faked union badges and forged instructions written on identical union note paper signed by forged signatures of the secretaries of the different unions which they are to visit in order to find out the class of man attending meetings and anything else that would matter in their eyes.'

I don't know how far this thing has gone but you may take it that if it hasn't gone beyond the initial stages it is because the enemy authorities are not certain of their ground. Their intention to do this is beyond doubt. I will not suggest to you how you can meet it as, of course, you will know far more about that aspect of the case than I do. But I would say that as a first step on your part a couple of reliable branch secretaries should be informed. I mean put on their guard with a view to immediate discovery when the attempt is made. From what I know of the way the enemy regard the unions, I am sure Transport would be the first body to be dealt with.[33]

Collins's mind worked at many levels. On the intelligence

front he kept his intelligence team busy with almost countless assignments. To Liam Tobin in spring 1921 he asked:

Have we any 'B' Men. I wonder if we can trace B who is said to have gone into the Joy [Mountjoy Jail] as a warder.[34]

Although in principle opposed to the use of hunger strikes as a form of protest, Collins none the less added his support to those imprisoned IRA men who undertook this perilous course. Terence MacSwiney's hunger strike afforded a noteworthy example of Collins's conduct in such instances. But there were also others. He was not unwilling to exploit such protests for their propaganda value in Ireland and abroad. In January 1920 he provided these orders to the Cork No. 1 Brigade's Acting Commandant.

I take it that their hunger strike was only undertaken after the making of a formal demand. Let me have a copy of this demand. You should arrange that the situation in the prison is kept in close touch with, and you should arrange for plenty of publicity to be given to the situation in the Cork press. Let me have a daily report on the situation for our own information here, and we will endeavour to have public attention kept on the matter.[35]

Collins's defence of the 'execution' of British spies and in some cases the callous murder of alleged civilian informers affords a look at his darker side during the War of Independence, even when the 'action' involved the shooting to death of an old woman, as in the case of one Mrs Lindsay. None the less, we also see a sense of regret on Collins's part for the slaying.

I was sorry about that . . . but she wasn't murdered in cold blood, she was executed. She lived in County Cork in the martial law area . . . she acted as an informer . . . she warned the police of an ambush and was the cause of military reprisals . . . so she was taken off by my men. [General] Strickland tried five men and was going to shoot them and did so. My fellows sent word if he did they'd shoot Mrs Lindsay whom they'd tried and found guilty as a spy and informer. The men were shot, so was Mrs Lindsay. But there is this about it, they should have referred it to me for decision, but did not do so . . . that's why I said I was sorry about it, as I don't think I'd have shot her on account of her age.[36]

He also took particular exception at IRA brigade commanders assigning intelligence officers to situations that would leave them at risk.

Provided orders given are carried out in a satisfactory manner, there should be no mistake. My orders do not permit an intelligence officer to go out on mail-raiding parties.[37]

As British military pressure on the IRA intensified during the first part of 1921, Collins and Mulcahy found themselves doing their best to activate sections of the country that had not displayed the revolutionary zeal of Dublin and south-west Munster, among other parts of the country. Large sections of the province of Connacht proved a source of vexation for Collins. On 15 April County Galway drew his ire in this communication to Mulcahy:

Connemara, west Galway, have been very bad, but I am having these fixed up on Tuesday next, and I think there will be no further complaint. Those who are not good have fled and the few left should be supported.[38]

One month later, Collins complained about the lack of detail in the reports on the few IRA actions occurring in the western counties of Mayo and Sligo.

It is very unfortunate a report [from West Mayo] has been delayed so long . . . as to their system of communication. There are some extracts which would valuably be sent [sic] . . . and other responsibilities to inform. It is almost too late to deal with them now . . . A great pity that arms were not captured. The report is very poor as they guess too much at the casualties. However, the great thing is that there is fighting in Mountbellew [Co. Galway] . . . Same type of report [from Co. Sligo] as always comes from there.[39]

The exchange of communications he carried out with the

IRA brigade commandants in his native County Cork were far more to his liking. Following an inquiry sent to him, Collins gave Liam Lynch, in his role as Commandant of the Cork No. 2 Brigade, the necessary approval to proceed with the reorganisation of his outfit, and as well empowered Lynch to intercede in a dispute involving the East Limerick and South Tipperary Brigades.

> You have full authority to act in accordance with your suggestion in regard to re-establishing and reorganising the Mitchelstown Company. You are further empowered to exclude from membership, for the present, any ex-officers or ex-Volunteers you may think undesirable. The names of any such wishing to join should be forwarded to us with a report. You will understand that this is necessary so that nothing unfair will be done to anybody . . . I enclose also to you a note for the Commandant of the East Limerick Brigade, also for the Adjutant of the South Tipperary Brigade, setting forth the suggestion you made. You will, I feel certain, be able to fix permanently the differences. . . . Please let me know how things progress and what arrangements are finally made. We are all glad that you feel yourself able to remain in the area [Galtee Mountains] for some time. The Adjutant of the South Tipperary Brigade is Maurice Crowe. Of course you know he is on the run, but you won't have any difficulty getting in touch with him.[40]

Matters involving discipline figured in Collins's communications with the Cork No. 2 Brigade the following April when he gave implicit approval for the disciplining of a rogue south Tipperary IRA officer with a penchant for conducting unauthorised raids on civilian households in north Cork.

> I am sure you will deal with the 'General' in proper style, and I am confident that the matter of ill-gotten goods will be amicably settled between the two brigades.[41]

A skill in the art of persuasion also characterised Collins's communications with brigade commandants, such as Terence MacSwiney, who had demonstrated their leadership ability on a number of fronts. The following offers testimony to that while also pointing to the competing interests between Collins's role as the IRA's Director of Intelligence and Adjutant General, as well as the degree to which even such active bodies as the Cork No. 1 Brigade were stretched when it came to assigning responsibilities for such areas as training, operations and intelligence gathering.

> Intelligence and information. I note and appreciate what you say, but the fact that many of the companies may be getting back to elementals in the matter of training and organisation should not prevent effect being given to the training in question right away. It simply means getting the circular into the hands of the different officers, getting them to see it in the proper light, and getting definite men to get on with the work.[42]

Collins's contact with IRA officers from his position at General Headquarters also included communication with those who were in prison and in many cases continuing their resistance from behind bars. Providing legal assistance and strategic advice to the commanding officer of a group of prisoners on protest at Cork Jail in April 1920 offers one example.

> 1. Your special dispatch received at 11.30 a.m. today. 2. You will immediately instruct solicitor to have statements from the four prisoners named. 3. Issue orders to the four prisoners on this matter. 4. I am sending instructions to the local brigade commander to send on a good solicitor . . . there should be no publication or attempt at publication in this matter until the solicitor has got the statements.[43]

As we have seen from the assassination of the thirteen British officers and ex-officers on Bloody Sunday, Michael Collins played a direct role in their selection for death. In fact, he went so far as to draw up a map pinpointing the residences of a number of them. But comments from Collins revealing what he actually said when giving out such grisly assignments to his 'squad' are harder to come by. More often than not the orders were given verbally and acknowledged later with a nod or even an attempt at denial on his part. Although the following account was told by Joe O'Reilly who served as Collins's aide-de-camp for much of the struggle and later during the Civil War, it is none the less useful given the clandestine nature of the subject matter involved. It conveys a vivid image of Collins's intensity during moments of stress, offering as well a glimpse of his sometimes violent temper. The episode in question marked the killing of RIC Sergeant Smith in Dublin. 'It was', Frank O'Connor wrote, 'Collins's first killing. Then as afterwards he did everything to avoid the necessity for it. With his strange sensitiveness he was haunted for days before by the thought of it. He was morose and silent. When the day of the killing came his staff saw for the first time the curious tension which would be repeated over and over again in the years to come. The same scene occurred so often that it became familiar.' O'Reilly would come forward to his leader with a report of the incident.[44] Collins would then jump up and, as O'Reilly demonstrated, he would

> . . . thrust his hands in his trousers pockets, and began to stamp about the room digging his heels in with a savagery that almost shook the house. Finally, he threw himself on to a sofa, picked up a newspaper which he pretended to read, tossed it aside after a few moments, and said, '. . . Jesus Christ Almighty, how often have I to tell ye . . ?'[45]

THE ANGLO-IRISH TRUCE

The Anglo-Irish Truce between the IRA and the Crown forces which took effect on 11 July 1921 proved a watershed for Michael Collins as well as for Ireland. Heretofore, Collins had been seen largely as one of the hardest of the hard men, unwilling to compromise with the British and determined instead to press forward with the IRA campaign of guerrilla warfare. His actions during the period which preceded his going to London as a leader of the Irish delegation sent to London in October 1921 affords us an opportunity to see how his views began to evolve as to what the most practical approach should be in securing Irish independence.

Collins's analysis of why the British Government decided so rapidly to reverse its policy of coercion in Ireland at mid-year

1921 and to instead seek a negotiated settlement offers a useful starting point. Although the views expressed in the following extract were uttered the following year, they none the less serve to illustrate how Collins tied his own change in outlook to the British policy reversal.

> But when the terror, growing ever more violent, and consequently ever more ineffective, failed to break the spirit of the Irish people —failed as it was bound to fail—concealment was no longer possible and the true explanation was blurted out when Lloyd George and Mr Bonar Law declared that their acts were necessary to destroy the authority of the Irish National Government which 'has all the symbols and all the realities of government'.
>
> When such a moment had been reached, there was only one course left open for the British Prime Minister—to invite the Irish leaders, 'the murderers', and heads of 'the murder gang' to discuss with him terms of peace . . . all accepted that invitation.[46]

Collins also offered an assessment to Éamon de Valera during the early stages of the Truce's implementation, particularly concerning the level of British military adherence to it, that was based on his own eyewitness experience and also drawing from his still very much intact intelligence gathering network.

> The spirit emanating from the enemy in Cork city and in parts of the country I visited is arrogant and provocative. They are trying to regard the position not as a truce but as a surrender on our part. For instance, the car in which I was travelling was held up in Clonakilty by regular troops, although they have no power whatever to undertake that action. . . . The first exciting incident I had was a few minutes after leaving Cork city going southwards. We very nearly were run into one of our own trenches. I said to the driver that if anything happened it would be the irony of fate.
>
> I would like you to know that while I was down in Cork yesterday, we intercepted messages from Bandon—that's the CI's office—Macroom, Bantry, Clonakilty. Castletownbere replied, 'roughly 1,500 males'. I can't judge what this could mean, unless it is an inquiry with a view to arrangements for a round-up. I think

it well that you should know this. That wire was handed in at Bandon at midday yesterday.[47]

At this early stage in the Truce, Collins evidenced a deep distrust of British intentions and offered advice to de Valera on what steps should be taken should there be a breakdown. Again, Collins's knowledge of British internal communications informed his recommendations.

Wires have also been issued to the effect that in the event of negotiations breaking down the enemy forces should be confined to attacks and will get further cipher as to the next step. Generally speaking, I fancy the idea is to have preparations made to attack us the moment they decide to finish their offers. I don't know whether anything really tangible has been offered up to the present, but I should say that in the final result it would be worthwhile stipulating that no matter how bad the terms are they would be submitted to a full meeting. You know my object in this.[48]

As the Truce progressed and direct contact took place between Sinn Féin and the British Government, Collins's correspondence with others shows the extent to which he monitored the signals emanating from Lloyd George, as well as a keen awareness of the British Prime Minister's own political difficulties. But this 17 August 1921 letter to Art O'Brien also reveals the road that Collins himself was travelling. Lloyd George appeared to be offering Ireland dominion status. The tone of Collins's letter—written some seven weeks before he would be heading up the Irish negotiating team in London with Arthur Griffith—suggests that by this stage it was an idea he was not averse to.

I think we may still be pleased enough with ourselves. Although Lloyd George's words looked big, you will notice a few peculiarities in his statement—peculiarities which do not look as if he felt himself very happy about the thoughts of resuming [the war]. His insistence on the dominion status offer is peculiar also . . . it may mean that by constantly repeating Dominion Home Rule he may reconcile his people to it.[49]

3

COLLINS THE MAN

C ollins's enthusiasm and passion for life were revealed even in a life which in its prime saw him living on the run.

Personal loyalty and trust also remained paramount to his existence. Often such loyalty went unrequited. Against the backdrop of the bitterness that would later develop between himself and Éamon de Valera over the Anglo-Irish Treaty, the fact that the two men had worked closely in the cause of Irish independence has become obfuscated with the passage of time. Particularly forgotten is that despite his myriad of obligations to the Irish independence effort, Michael Collins also provided dedicated assistance to de Valera—the man he referred to as the 'Chief', as did others who worked closely with the President of the Dáil Government. During de Valera's almost two years spent in the United States from 1919 to 1920 Collins also made a particular point of caring for the Irish leader's family, indeed becoming something of a surrogate father to de Valera's children. It was a display of kindness that de Valera's wife never forgot.

Collins's personal assistance rendered to de Valera continued after his return from the United States. On 19 April 1921 he informed de Valera that one of his associates would 'look after the clothes tomorrow and get the car to take them out'. 'Whether you are settled or not', he noted, 'the other suit might as well go there too, mightn't it?' De Valera's housing needs were also attended to by Collins out of personal concern as much as out of any peripheral obligation as Minister for Finance.

> I am afraid it looks as if the furnished house were off [*sic*]. The lady who called was asked any amount of pointed questions, so much so that she had difficulty in bestowing suitable answers. She does not think she will hear any further on the matter, therefore he is going on at once with buying the house. . . . There is another place I am going to enquire about today. If it's any good I'll let you know.[1]

As the situation evolved towards the attainment of a political settlement and away from armed conflict against Britain, the differences between Collins and de Valera became more pronounced, even prior to the signing of the Anglo-Irish Treaty. Indeed Collins's resentment at having been sent to do what he called 'the impossible' in England was shared by Arthur Griffith. Griffith, a man whom Collins long respected, grew to become a close friend. Later Griffith would refer to Collins as 'the man who won the war'. Here Collins speaks of how he and Griffith pondered the untenable situation in which they found themselves in London and of his trust in Griffith, and at the same time his resentment towards Erskine Childers, whom he and Griffith both believed had been handpicked by de Valera to spy on them whilst serving as secretary to the Irish delegation.

> . . . Rather the years that have gone before with all their attendant risks than the atmosphere that is part of this conference. Who should we trust—even on my own side of the fence? Griffith. Beyond Griffith no one. As for C [Childers] it would be better that he led the delegation. He is sharp to realise how things will have due effect in Dublin—and acts accordingly.[2]

Later he alluded further to his friend John O'Kane about the close bond that had developed between Griffith and himself, while at the same time admitting the soft spot he continued to harbour for Cathal Brugha, the latter's personal animosity toward him notwithstanding.

> Griffith and I had a lonely meeting—a house almost empty of

customers—and talked and talked. He confessed that he was far from well and asked me to assume leadership of our party, even if unofficial. He and I recognise that if such a thing were official it would provide bullets for the unmentionables. I agreed poor Griffith is in poor health and further burdens will do no more than grossly worsen his burdens. We came to the topic for the thousandth [sic] time of the Dublinites. I have often said that Brugha commanded respect and I still say the same. I respect a fighter and B [Brugha] is one. Only he is misguided. Yet even in enmity he is capable of sincerity—which is more than I can say of the others.[3]

None the less, the insights into himself that Collins offered from London also included a plea for openness to his fiancée Kitty Kiernan. The letter, written on his birthday, 16 October 1921, also evidences his desire to remain unaffected from a rash of favourable publicity given him in the British press.

Please always say to me what you think, not what I'd like you to think. That's the only way to get a proper understanding, and if I don't like what you say, then it's my look out. You realise what I mean—don't you Kit? And I hope you'll see a close link when you look at the real photograph and see the more vivid stripes. . . . You'll have seen all the praise and flattery that has been showered on me since I came here and have been publicly known. You will know I hope that they leave me untouched just as their dispraise and their blame did. All the same to me. That upper lip of mine has been called on to do much scornful upturning since I've seen you.[4]

THE PRESS

In what had by then become the age of modern communications, with the printed word able to reach mass millions through improved means of communications on a daily basis, it is not surprising that Michael Collins with his 'Scarlet Pimpernel' image had become a figure during the War of Independence that commanded considerable interest from journalists, including those covering the Anglo-Irish conflict for the American press. One such journalist covered Collins, Carl Ackerman of the *Philadelphia Ledger*. In 1920 and 1921 Ackerman filed several stories based on interviews with Collins 'in the field'. The following revisions were forwarded by Collins to Ackerman on 6 April 1921 prior to the publication of the interview.

> Enclosed herewith is the story as I would like it to appear. You will observe that I have made some few slight alterations in the form, and have made a few slight corrections. . . . Page 5. The opening sentence on your draft was not what I said. 'We know those men were not on the jobs' is the form used. Please note this specially. . . . Otherwise I think everything is clear, except that I would like to draw your attention to one serious error into which you have fallen. I do not know any Sinn Féiners who think Macready kind and human and meaning to be fair. We believe he is here to do a dirty job for a dirty enemy and he and his satellites are acting up to their terms of reference with apparent satisfaction . . . If you come to Ireland again take care you do not have this letter on you when you run into one of the English ambushes. It would ruin you in their eyes and I fear all your American citizenship would not prevail against their fury.[5]

Given the efficiency with which Collins's intelligence team operated, it is ironic that Carl Ackerman was in fact a British informant. Unknown to Collins, or anyone around him, his letter was in fact almost immediately forwarded by Ackerman to the authorities at Dublin Castle. Sir Hamar Greenwood, the British Chief Secretary for Ireland, in turn, sent the correspondence to Lloyd George with the comment: 'This has been given us by Ackerman. We could use it.' In effect, Ackerman had little to fear from the British side.[6]

COLLINS'S JUDGMENT OF OTHERS

Collins's assessments of those he dealt with across the table on the British side during the Anglo-Irish Conference from October to December 1921 are revealing both for the personal insight they give us on his attitude towards his opponents and also because they shed further light on his highly analytical mind. We see here in these assessments of Lloyd George, Winston Churchill, Hamar Greenwood and others the judgment that Collins brought to bear as Director of Intelligence during the War of Independence and how these skills in assessing people were still being finely honed.

On Lloyd George:

Born poor, is therefore shrewd. Was lawyer, therefore crafty. Nicknamed the 'Welsh Wizard' and for good reason. Has a great deal of craft in his political methods, in his diplomatic approaches. Trusts that his fatherly air and benevolence will overcome all obstacles—craft again. 'Now Michael . . .', he says, or 'Now Mick'. On formal occasions it is 'Now Mr Collins . . .' Not sure how far he can go with me. Confided that Arthur G. [Griffith] was altogether too dour for dealings. That Barton was suspicious of him as I am. But that Duffy and Duggan are pigeons for the plucking. Would sell his nearest and dearest for political prestige. '14–'18 war good and bad for him. Hopes this affair will win him political prestige—which apparently he definitely needs.[7]

On Winston Churchill:

Don't know quite whether he would be a crafty enemy in friendship. Outlook: political gain, nothing else. Will sacrifice all for political gain. Studies, I imagine, the details carefully—thinks about his constituents, effect of so and so on them. Inclined to be bombastic. Full of ex-officer jingo or similar outlook. Don't actually trust him.[8]

On Hamar Greenwood:

A man who earns my personal detestation. Feeling reciprocated, I would say. Canadian. Bombastic. Overriding. Could settle this issue in one day—in favour of Britain.[9]

On Austen Chamberlain:

Don't like Chamberlain. Difficult man. Son of Joseph C. Never informal. Says one thing and apparently does another. Middle of the road man. Plays safe. Educated Rugby public school and Cambridge. Probably thinks of G. [Griffith] and myself as heathens. Equal with Duffy, politically and otherwise.[10]

While the comments that follow relate to his collective view of the British career politicians that are represented by the British side of the London Conference, they none the less offer valuable insights into Collins's views on politics and politicians in general. They also afford us a window on how Collins viewed himself, the qualities of straightforwardness and candour he valued. And they reveal a certain anomaly in that elsewhere we see that while distrusting politics and politicians, he also trusted the will of the people and the democratic process. Indeed, it was while trying to develop democratic institutions for an independent Ireland that Collins died.

Whenever I think of politics, I think of the false air which is a part of most politicians.

However much he may blind the public, and even himself, into thinking that he is for party and country, it does not blind me into thinking the same way. To be a politician one needs to keep tongue in cheek for all of the day and most of the night; one needs to have the ability to say one thing and mean another; one needs to be abnormally successful at the 'art' of twisting the truth. Can you wonder that I think and think yet never manage to achieve peace of mind? In my time I have told men and women what I thought of them. I've cursed them—and they understand me all the more for it. But what can one say to a politician? Knowing it is more than possible that one's words will be taken out of context, twisted and warped, shaped into a lie, and be flung back into my teeth. I do not in the least care for the false atmosphere of these discussions.[11]

Collins also, not surprisingly, held strong views about key figures in Irish history. Of Daniel O'Connell, one of the icons of nineteenth-century Irish nationalism, Collins's judgment can be said to have been harsh.

O'Connell was a product of the Ireland that arose out of this perversion [Catholic Emancipation for an Ireland represented solely at Westminster]. Prompted by the Young Irelanders and urged on by the zeal of the people, stirred for the moment to national consciousness by the teaching of Davis, he talked of national liberty, but he did nothing to win it. He was a follower and not a leader of people. He feared any movement of a revolutionary nature. Himself a Gaelic speaker, he adopted the English. . . . He would have Ireland merely a prosperous province of Britain with no national distinctiveness. Generally speaking, he acquiesced in a situation which was bringing upon the Irish nation spiritual decay.[12]

But for the Young Ireland movement and Thomas Davis in particular Collins held a special reverence. We see in the following assessment of Davis and the work of Young Ireland much that Collins sought to emulate in his own patriotic outlook.

The Young Irelanders, of whom Thomas Davis was the inspiration, were the real leaders. They saw and felt more deeply and aimed more truly. Davis spoke to the soul of the sleeping nation—drunk with the waters of forgetfulness. He sought to unite the whole people. He fought against sectarianism and all the other causes which divided them. He saw that unless we were Gaels we were not a nation. When he thought of the nation he thought of the men and women of the nation. He knew that unless they were free Ireland could not be free and to fill them again with pride in their nation he sang to them of the splendour of old Ireland, of their heroes, of their language, of the strength of unity, of the glory of noble strife, of the beauties of the land . . . That was the National Gospel. 'Educate that you may be free', he said.

Similarly of Arthur Griffith and William Rooney, the founders of the Sinn Féin movement, he also spoke glowingly.

The Sinn Féin movement was both economic and national, meeting therefore the two evils produced by the Union. Inspired by Arthur Griffith and William Rooney, it grew to wield enormous educational and spiritual power. It organised the country. It promoted what came to be known as the 'Irish Ireland Policy'. It preached the re-creation of Ireland built upon the Gael. It penetrated in Belfast and north-east Ulster and was doing encouraging educational work, and was making the national revival general when the war broke out in 1914. If that work could have been completed, the freedom which has been won [by

the Anglo-Irish Treaty, 1921] would have been completed. . . .
The Sinn Féin movement was not militant, but the militant
movement existed within it, and by its side. It had for its
advocates the two mightiest figures that have appeared in the
whole present movement—Tom Clarke and Sean MacDermott.
The two movements worked in perfect harmony. Rooney
preached language and liberty; he inspired all whom he met with
national pride and courage . . . Rooney spoke as a prophet.[13]

4

COLLINS AND FINANCE

Michael Collins's ability to comprehend complex financial issues during the early days of the Irish Free State has been well documented in Ronan Fanning's impressive study of the Irish Department of Finance. Many of the financial underpinnings of an independent Ireland were founded on initiatives that Collins in fact set in place as Minister for Finance in the Dáil Government during the War of Independence. Indeed, the passage of time has only served to reconfirm the contribution made by Collins to an independent Ireland in the public finance front. Garret FitzGerald, who was twice the Irish Republic's Taoiseach during the 1980s and a former Minister for Foreign Affairs, has emphasised Collins's invaluable role in this arena.[1]

While Collins and Sinn Féin received little satisfaction from either President Woodrow Wilson or the Paris Peace Conference in the way of recognition of the Irish Republic in 1919, the substance of the arguments Collins prepared that May for public consumption by a visiting US panel to Dáil Éireann as to the extent of Britain's over-taxation of Ireland and its efforts to cripple the Irish economy, Collins's statement read like a bill of indictment before a court of law.

England stands arraigned with having through her financial machinations:
1. Overtaxed us to the extent of at least £400,000.

2. Drained our capital to the extent of (at a moderate estimate, as already set forth) £1,000,000,000.

3. Destroyed flourishing industries and generally retarded our industrial development.

4. Banished some million of our population and made the remainder 'pay' as Grattan said they would pay, 'the price of their own enslavement'.[2]

That Collins dealt with complex questions of finance for the Revolutionary Irish Republican Government and the Free State, in the case of the former while also on the run from the British Government, and in the case of the latter in the midst of great division in the country after the Anglo-Irish Treaty, must be underscored. His efforts as Minister for Finance earned the accolades of Arthur Griffith who, as Acting President, stated that Collins had 'accomplished one of the most extraordinary feats in the country's history'. By the end of June 1920, the Dáil actually was oversubscribed by £40,000 despite what Griffith termed 'the most determined opposition of England'.[3]

On 17 July 1920 Collins asked the Dáil to close the raising of the Dáil Loan. On that day the effort stood at £340,000, £281,000 of that having been raised in Ireland, and £59,000 in the USA. He submitted figures showing a balance of more than £260,000 after expenses.[4] It was a remarkable accomplishment for a *de facto* government operating not only within the shadow of the British Empire but also up against a full frontal assault by that Empire to undermine it. By September the Dáil Loan was closed out at a figure of £1,370,165 raised. Remarkably, more than one-third of that amount came from the province of Munster. Owing to a great extent to Éamon de Valera's efforts in the United States, the September figures also showed that an additional £505,000 was raised in that country.

Collins was clear in the remarks accompanying the submission of these figures to the Dáil as to what the net result of the proper distribution of this money would mean:

[It would] reduce England's profit on holding the country; to transfer the power and advantage which the collection of revenues gives to a government; to utilise that power for the mobilisation and direction of Irish peace efforts against the

41

Enemy—in short to press the national riches, as well as the national sentiment, into the service of Ireland. These are the national aims we have in view today. They will be achieved gradually, but achieved they will be.[5]

During the War of Independence the full range of Collins's contribution in this important arena included: the raising of the Dáil Loan to sustain the Revolutionary Government; the provision of funds raised by this and other sources to separate departments; while also ensuring funding for the purchase of weapons to make possible the IRA's campaign. With this came the responsibility of protecting by an elaborate mechanism of accounting those funds from seizure by the British authorities, including the actual conversion of some of those funds into gold bullion and hiding it in various locations around Dublin including a hidden compartment in a fireplace in a house owned by Batt O'Connor. Perhaps most amazing, given the fact that he was operating a finance department for a government outlawed by the Crown, is the fact that Collins also engaged in overseas transactions as a way of sheltering the funds. In February 1921 Collins provided Éamon de Valera with a detailed analysis of his proposal to invest Dáil funds in a Radio telegraphic agency in France at a price of five million francs. His proposal had apparently originated with Sean T. O'Kelly during his travels in France on behalf of the Republic. In his correspondence with de Valera, Collins showed his grasp of complex details.

From the financial side, the report attached is complete and expresses my view exactly. Briefly it may be stated the proposition is that we invest 5,000,000 francs and the position then would be:

1. Immobilisations A/C 2,301,612 francs.
2. Profit and loss A/C 1,418,113 francs.
3. Cash on hand (proceeds of calls due) 1,545,000 francs.

In other words, we would be giving away roughly 3,720,000 francs for a very doubtful venture. In addition it is to be noted that . . . a proposal for expending £200,000 to extend the business— at this point . . . However I am not at all satisfied that even at the above price we would have complete control. In my opinion the thing is financially unstable and doubtful and in that ground alone

I recommend that we take no action and that Sean T. [*sic*] be informed on the lines of the secretary's memo and the financial memo.[6]

Two weeks earlier when the idea of purchasing the telegraphic company was first raised with him by de Valera and a meeting between one of the principals of the company with the Minister for Finance was suggested, Collins issued this terse reply.

It is rather absurd sending along that L'Abbe chap [*sic*] until we have the particulars I have asked for. An opportunity of checking these would have been of value, but of course there won't be such an opportunity now as we shall simply get the particulars verbally from him.[7]

In the end de Valera heeded Collins's advice. The Dáil did not purchase the telegraphic company. Later in this section we will see other examples of Collins's financial prowess.

In time of war Collins, the Republic's Minister for Finance, also made use of his double role as the IRA's Director of Intelligence to ruthlessly protect the finances of the Republic. A classic example of that ruthlessness is provided by the treatment meted out under Collins's orders to Resident Magistrate Alan Bell of the RIC. To Bell had fallen the task of finding the sources of the deposits in various Irish banks where Collins had placed the proceeds from the National Loan and other revenues raised under various names. On the morning of 26 March 1920, while on his way to work in a Dublin tram, Bell was assassinated in full public view by members of Collins's handpicked hit squad. Of all the British agents dispatched to and within Ireland, Bell had come closest to uncovering Collins's complex financial apparatus.

THE DÁIL LOAN

The Dáil or National Loan was perhaps the single most important fundraising source for providing the financial wherewithal for both the War of Independence and the day-to-day functioning of the Dáil Government. It was largely conceived of and implemented by Michael Collins with the help of an apparatus he had also assembled in Ireland, the United States, Britain and elsewhere. For nearly two years in the United States between 1919 and 1920 Éamon de Valera, in his role as President of the Republic, also played an important part raising funds for the loan through his work with Clan na Gael and other Irish separatist support organisations at well attended rallies and fundraising events across the American continent. But it was Collins who put the apparatus for the Dáil Loan scheme together, who oversaw its operation and held the greatest sway in the disbursement of its funds.

The Dáil Loan effort was initiated at a session of Dáil Éireann in the autumn of 1919. It was placed directly under Collins's purview as Minister for Finance. In all, from its beginning to its completion in July 1920, over £1 million had been raised in support of the Irish independence effort at home and abroad. While the loan was not the only source of funds available to the IRA and Dáil Éireann, it provided revenue on a scale that no other structure did. The following is an extract of the prospectus co-signed by Michael Collins and Arthur Griffith, the latter serving as Acting President during de Valera's absence. The statement is as such a social document outlining a view for Ireland's development that is consistent with the Democratic Programme announced by Dáil Éireann early in 1919.

> The Loan, both internal and external, will be utilised solely in the interests of Ireland—an indivisible entity. It will be used to unshackle Irish Trade and Commerce, and give them free access to the markets of the world; it will be used to provide Ireland with an efficient Consular service; it will be used to end the plague of emigration, by providing land for the landless and work for the workless; it will be used to determine the industrial and commercial resources of our country and to arrange for their development; it will be used to encourage and develop the long neglected Irish Sea fisheries, and to promote the re-afforestation of our barren wastes; it will be available for, and will be applied to, all purposes which tend to make Ireland morally and materially strong and self-supporting.[8]

A promotional film on the Dáil Loan for distribution in Irish cinemas promoting the undertaking shows a confident-looking

Collins seated at a desk taking subscriptions from the widow of Tom Clarke and the mother of Patrick and Willie Pearse. The film was actually screened in the cinemas of Dublin before its eventual seizure by British authorities. By mid-October 1919 the British Government had made it clear by its actions that it viewed the loan effort as a major threat to British rule. In December of that year Collins informed de Valera, still in America, addressing him 'My Dear Dev', of the enormous pressures the loan effort faced.

> The situation has been getting more and more difficult lately. The arrests at the Dáil offices were a very serious handicap from a routine point of view. I fear there is no one here now who gives you, or any of your assistants, any real news as to how things are developing. I am doubtless as much to blame as anybody, but I have at least the shadow of a good excuse. I may say, however, that my own activity is progressing fairly in the circumstances. The total net amount of money subscribed to the loan to date is about £30,000, making applications the extent of about £35,000. You will understand that this is not very satisfactory, but hindrances have been simply enormous. Indeed, at the present moment, the main enemy objective is directed to secure the failure of the enterprise.. Yet that objective will not be reached for although things have been slow, they have been sure and the promises made throughout the country and reported to me up to the present total something in the neighbourhood of £100,000. Advertising is impossible practically, meetings are impossible practically, movements of prominent Sinn Féiners are greatly interfered with, so that everything has to be done quietly.[9]

Two months later, the assessment he sent to de Valera was far more optimistic despite the British Government's coercive efforts against the loan. Collins's letter also reflected his appreciation for the great success that the President of the Irish Republic's efforts had been meeting in the United States.

> The enemy Government quickly realised that the economic policy of the Dáil was as great a danger to them as its political policy, that in fact the elected Government of Ireland stood for social and economic deliverance no less than for political

deliverance. Without finance, however, the policy would be inoperative. The enemy must at all costs, therefore, prevent our getting the necessary funds. . . . His military and armed police smashed up meetings called to support the loan. They suppressed newspapers, and removed their machinery, if mention were made of the loan Prospectuses and literature was seized in the Post Office where discovered. . . . Our people in distributing leaflets and prospectuses had to use the byways and not infrequently had to cross country to avoid enemy forces. Men were put in jail for requesting applications and men were put in jail for making an application. People found in possession of documents relating to the loan were put in jail, and the entire male Head Office Staff was put in jail as an 'Illegal Assembly'. The Head Office itself was closed by the military.

Yet all attempts have singularly failed . . . We have sent out throughout the length and breadth of Ireland 500,000 copies of the Prospectus, and 2,000,000 leaflets, and a special letter to over 50,000 individuals. . . . In return the response has been splendid. From the constituency of West Limerick they have sent us £10,000 . . . from mid-Cork, remote and mountainous with no town of any size, they have sent over £5,000, and there too the work is still going on . . . In the Castlebar district they have collected £2,500 and other constituencies in Connaght are doing the same. To illustrate Ulster I will quote two places— North Fermanagh and East Down. Their figures are £3,000 and £4,000 respectively. They will not be long Unionist . . . These figures indicate a very creditable achievement. They assure final success of our efforts here.[10]

None the less, the safe administration of the loan continued to provide as great a challenge to Collins as raising the money itself since he was under the constant pressure of British raids. In the autumn of 1919 he explained the slowness of his response in a communication to Terence MacSwiney, the principal organiser of the Dail Loan effort in Cork:

. . . you will forgive me for not replying sooner, but I have been extremely rushed as a result of raids and seizure of correspondence in various parts of the country . . . The Head Foci seems to be the only place where no documents were got.[11]

Collins as a six-year-old boy in Clonakilty, Co. Cork

A rare early photograph of Collins in Volunteer uniform, probably taken before the Easter Rising (courtesy of Ita O'Connor)

Anti-Treatyite prisoners in civilian clothes being taken into custody by troops of the Provisional Government, following the bombardment of the Four Courts, Dublin, June 1922 (from Kilmainham Gaol Museum, courtesy of The Office of Public Works)

Collins flanked by Tom Cullen and Liam Tobin, two key members of his intelligence squad, Dublin 1921 (from Kilmainham Gaol Museum, courtesy of The Office of Public Works)

Collins in London during the Anglo-Irish Conference, October–
December 1921

Signatures of both the British and Irish Delegations to the Anglo-Irish Conference, October–December 1921

The Cabinet Room at No. 10 Downing Street, where Collins and his colleagues met the British side, headed by David Lloyd George

Poster for rally held at
Naas, Co. Kildare

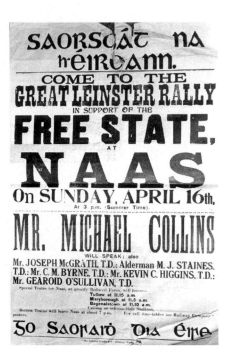

Collins talks with members of the Kilkenny hurling team before a
match at Croke Park, Dublin 1921

Collins after Arthur Griffith's funeral in Glasnevin, August 1922. He was now both Chairman of the Provisional Government and Commander-in-Chief of the Provisional Army, but he had only ten more days to live.

Lady Hazel Lavery followed by her husband, the painter Sir John Lavery, exits the Pro Cathedral, Dublin after Collins's funeral mass.

Collins's body at Shanakiel Hospital, Cork

Collins also saw the efficacy behind a series of high profile public endorsements of the Dail Loan scheme, including members of the Catholic hierarchy. Dr Fogarty, the Bishop of Killaloe, was one who came forward to do so enthusiastically. But there were others such as Dr Cohalan of Cork who proved more elusive. Collins appears to have placed a high priority on Terence MacSwiney winning the bishop's endorsement of the loan effort as underscored by a number of directives he sent him on the matter. One such communication was sent on 29 March 1920.

> You will also appreciate my desire that you should lose no opportunity of having that interview with his Lordship. The point I already made about the moral value we may get from same is becoming more and more obvious as the days go on.[12]

Three weeks later, with Cohalan still not an endorsee, Collins reiterated to MacSwiney the importance of engaging Cohalan.

> If you have not seen his Lordship by this time, I wonder if you would make it your special business to interview him in priority to any other engagement whatever . . . You will forgive me . . . if I have been unduly stressing this matter with you, but I have given up hope of Liam [De Roiste] going to see him. Mr Childers took an introduction from me [regarding the Republican Land Bank] and had no difficulty in seeing him.[13]

MacSwiney replied to Collins a few days later having by this time met Cohalan. He was met with the bishop's refusal, however. Collins would not take no for an answer. Again he pressed MacSwiney.

> I think I understand his Lordship's point of view, but frankly I am surprised that he did not meet you more readily . . . However, I have not the slightest doubt that he will be as good as his word, or—if I may use the expression—better than his word.[14]

But the matter was left unresolved, while MacSwiney apparently contemplated something more drastic than moral suasion for the bishop.[15]

But despite these obstacles and the threat of official murder in addition to arrest and censorship, Collins doggedly persisted in getting the job of organising and administering the National Loan done. He devised systems for hiding receipts from police and military raids, and established an elaborate communications network around the loan. As his biographer Frank O'Connor has written, 'It was no job for the easygoing man, and Collins cracked the whip. Many men in the country parishes remember him only as organiser of the loan; and how they trembled before him. Alibis were in vain; he knew the capacity of every townland.'[16]

It was a confident Michael Collins who on 7 July 1920 publicly announced the decision of Dáil Éireann that the loan would be closed to subscriptions, effective one week later. At the time of the release of this statement the loan total stood at £295,000.

> . . . after that date no further money can be accepted for this issue of the loan unless it can be shown that the application in respect of such payment was made prior to the said date. Other than such amounts, any money tendered is to be credited to the Self-determination Fund.[17]

In the end the Dáil Loan raised some £450,000, two-thirds of that amount in Ireland, with the balance raised largely by de Valera in the United States. Given the conditions which Collins and his loyal cadre of associates throughout the country laboured, it was not an exaggeration when Arthur Griffith as Acting President proclaimed in Dáil Éireann on 29 June 1920 that 'The Minister for Finance has accomplished one of the most extraordinary feats in the country's history.' By that point the loan was actually oversubscribed by some £40,000, with £171,000 raised in Collins's home province of Munster alone, amounting to more than one-third of the total.[18]

In sum these efforts served dramatically to help make the Dáil Government more than a debating society in which resolutions were passed. It enabled Sinn Féin to take substantial steps to undermine British rule in much of the country, including the establishment of the Dáil Courts, the setting up of diplomatic missions in seven countries, in addition to an ambassador in Washington and consular offices in four American cities. It enabled Sinn Féin to conduct their own propaganda campaign at home and abroad, while also providing significant funding for the purchase of weapons and ammunition for the Irish Republican Army. The timing of the loan and its success was also crucial given that it occurred at a time when both the British military presence, including the introduction of the Black and Tans, and its coercive efforts in the country increased exponentially. Without the financial wherewithal to conduct a revolution and help develop institutions to undermine British rule at the same time, there would probably be little basis for a historian to write about an Irish War of Independence. It was with considerable prescience then that Collins wrote to Art O'Brien in London in February 1920 and offered this assessment of the heightened British effort to crush the revolt in Ireland.

[The Government had] seen clearly that the success of the loan is one of our steps to economic freedom—it is the first token of release from the strangle grip which English money—or rather our own money in English hands—holds us in.[19]

STEWARDING PUBLIC FUNDS

Despite his years on the run from arrest or worse during the War of Independence, Collins kept detailed records of his activities as Minister for Finance. After de Valera's return from the United States at the end of 1920, the record indicates that he also kept the President apprised on a regular basis of his activities. A memo from Collins to de Valera dated 7 January 1921, dealing with monthly payments to Dáil Ministries, is useful in showing his grasp of financial details and the rigour of the methods he employed in the disbursement of public funds. Collins's communication came in response to a request from de Valera asking that he explain 'the details of the arrangements which you make with the heads of departments on money matters generally'.[20]

The procedure for dealing with these is that on the last day of each month an estimate is given to his Department by each of the other Departments [sic] of the amount required to carry on during the coming month. Together with this account a statement I submitted showing the items of expenditure during the past month, and the balance in hand, if any . . . If a Department receives any money by way of revenue or otherwise it does not go to the credit of that Department but is included in the account and consequently goes to the credit of the Trustees at the end of the month—what I mean is, any receipts are not spent by the Department. Of course there are only one or two Departments that have any receipts at all.[21]

For Collins to carry out his financial responsibilities, securing his base of operations became paramount. Hugh O'Kennedy, a legal adviser to the Dáil Government, has stated that although 'daring and skill succeeded wonderfully in enabling the Ministers and their staffs to execute functions to a greater or lesser degree, files of papers were sometimes seized, and were always in danger of seizure'.[22] Collins found a way to circumvent these difficulties, perhaps better than most. After a raid in 1920 on Sinn Féin's offices in Dublin, he purchased a house for the purpose of allowing him to oversee the Dáil Loan initiative. Soon after, he purchased a second house, this time at No. 76 Harcourt Street. In that and in yet another in Parnell Street he had his trusted friend Batt O'Connor construct a hidden closet within the walls of the homes where valuable documents were hidden. O'Connor, as Ronan Fanning has noted, also 'buried the bulk of Collins's precious gold reserves which totalled £25,000 in a baby's coffin under the floor of his own house at 1 Brendan Road, Donnybrook.'[23] Collins also conducted his financial work from offices at Nos 22, 28 and 29 Mary Street, within a special compartment of a draper's shop at 28/29, and No. 3 St Andrew's Street, along with still other locations.

Collins was equally determined to safeguard the functioning of the Department of Finance from assault from within the Dáil Government as he was from the British. On 17 September 1920 he told a private session of the Dáil of his support for the levying of an 'audit fee' to be paid to the Department by the local government authorities. But he was more than cool to a proposal that the Department would be forced to rely on the local authorities for its administrative costs.

The suggestion that the Department be financed by the local bodies was wrong from every point of view. It would make the

Department subsidiary to the local bodies, any one of which could stop payment at any time, and thereby weaken the control of the Department.[24]

Testimony to Collins's commitment to financial accountability is reflected in a year end statement he submitted to Dáil Éireann detailing receipts and expenditures right down to the penny for the half-year covering 1 May to 31 December 1920.

It will be noted that the total receipts [from] all sources allowing for accrued interest, refunds and transfers from the USA, amounted to £335,115:15:0, while the gross expenditures amounted to £51,905:17:7, an excess of receipts over expenditures of £283,210:7:3, which adds to the amount of £176,637:10:10 brought into accounts made a total gross amount expended at that date of £458,787: 8: 5.[25]

Collins's report also noted that for the month of November 1920, a sum totalling £29,805 had arrived from the United States.[26] But despite Collins's proven ability to balance the Dáil Government's books and to help generate funds, the increasing effectiveness of the enemy in capturing IRA officers and prominent Sinn Féiners is reflected in this note he sent on 21 January 1921 on the matter of receipts for the Dáil Loan in mid-Cork.

I have a large number of Loan receipts and I am at a loss to know where I should send them. Most of the people with whom I was in touch during the time of the loan activity are now either dead or in jail.[27]

Stories of Collins's own ability to avoid arrest or worse during the War of Independence are the stuff of legend. The incidents ran the gamut of Collins escaping through skylights, jumping from one roof to another, hiding in chimneys only to leave them hours later covered in soot, to making safe but harried get-aways on an old but reliable bicycle he owned. In June 1921 Collins alluded to the narrowness of some of those escapes in a memorandum to Éamon de Valera.

I may tell you between ourselves that the escape on Thursday was nothing to four or five escapes I have had since. They ran me very close for a good while on Sunday evening. The engineering friend is a nuisance—he won't do what he is told and take care of himself.[28]

But the financial matters addressed by Collins also took on a personal note. On 7 January 1921, in a response to a communication he had received earlier that day from de Valera in which the President queried Collins about a complaint he had received from Cathal Brugha on the basis that he had failed to release a sum of £500 which the Dáil had voted his Ministry for Defence for propaganda purposes, Collins offered further evidence of the rift that existed between himself and Brugha. That the date of the incident involved is almost a full year before Collins found himself up against both de Valera and Brugha over the Anglo-Irish Treaty is also noteworthy.

I have received no notification of a special vote of 500 pounds for M/D [sic]. I am inquiring from the Secretary as to why he did not notify me in the usual way. I have no knowledge of the matter myself, and in any case the M/D did not make application.[29]

Collins informed de Valera that he was treating an amount of £224 that the latter had brought back from the United States as a 'remittance from the USA'. He also apprised him about the President's own wife's transportation needs—evidence of how many details Collins was forced to deal with on a myriad of topics, often all at once. This last item also evidences that the manner in which Mrs de Valera had come to depend on Collins for support during her husband's prolonged absence in America still continued to some extent after his return.

I received word from Mrs Dev. [sic] to alter the car from 12:30 to 2:30 so she will be out at 3:00. The car will call for her in sufficient time to bring her into town to whatever train she desires back, that is, she wants to go back tomorrow night. I think it is wise that she should go back as her absence might be more remarkable than anything else.[30]

The end of the year would find him confronting different burdens and far removed from the de Valera household. In playing a leadership role on the Irish delegation to the October –December 1921 Anglo-Irish Conference in London, to Collins fell the responsibility of defending the Irish position against over-taxation by the Crown under any settlement. The exchange on 19 October 1921 early on in the negotiations between Collins and several British Ministers including Secretary of State for War Sir Laming Worthington-Evans and Chancellor of the Exchequer Sir Robert Horne, among others, is instructive not simply for Collins's ability to engage them in debate alone, but for the substance of his argument.

Worthington-Evans: Having regard to the relative taxable capacities of Great Britain and Ireland, what is the fair proportion which each should pay towards the Debt and Pensions, and on what basis should these be capitalised?

Collins: Our desire is to get a definite figure. That is our whole purpose. We want to draw a line.

Worthington-Evans: When you get your figure you can raise any argument you like. We give you your X and Y.

Collins: I will put some arguments that may surprise you.

Worthington-Evans: Mr Collins will never surprise me again. We would like to have a statement of your counter-claims. Could you put these in now? . . .

Collins: According to my figures our counter-claim works out at £3,940,000,000.

Horne: I suppose that dates from the time of Brian Boru. How much did we owe you then?

Collins: Oh no. It is the capital sum since the Act of Union.[31]

THE FINANCES OF THE NEW STATE

As Minister for Finance as well as Chairman of the Provisional Government established on 14 January 1922, despite the efforts of the Anti-Treatyites to the contrary, Collins set about raising revenue to underwrite the new, native Irish Government. Under the new office of Finance and General which Collins created early in 1922, five prior Treasury

Departments under the prior Irish executive were subsumed, as well as twenty-five other departments previously under the jurisdiction of Dublin Castle.[32] But although Collins would resign in the midst of the Irish Civil War as Chairman of the Provisional Government and Minister for Finance to become Commander-in-Chief of the Free State Army, his presence continued to be felt over the Cabinet and the entire government.

Two days after resigning from the Cabinet in what was ironically the first anniversary of the 1921 Anglo-Irish Truce, Collins issued a proposed loyalty oath for the members of all government departments. The effort, modelled after the British Official Secrets Act, demonstrated how determined he was to weed out less than loyal members of the Irish civil service.

1. Do you promise faithfully to serve the government elected by the Irish people in a position of _____?
2. Have you ever taken any part directly or indirectly in the armed conflict against the Irish Government?
3. Have you helped in any way or aided or abetted any forces levying war against the Irish Government?
4. Are you in any way using your official position for the purpose of conveying information to the Opponents [*sic*] of the Government, or are you in any way conveying information regarding official matters to any person outside the Government service?
5. Have you read the Official Secrets Act, and are you prepared loyally to abide by the terms of same?[33]

An example of what Collins had in mind in the way of ensuring financial accountability within the mechanisms of the new Irish state, had there not been a civil war and, in particular, had he lived, was provided on 15 May 1922 when he asked that all Ministers of the Provisional Government operate 'with an outline of the policy to be adopted after the elections, including reforms, economies, extensions and improvements'. A memorandum with which he said he would provide the Ministers on these topics was never finished, however, due to more demanding pressures.[34]

5

COLLINS: DEMOCRATIC POLITICS, PARTITION AND THE NORTH

Michael Collins had already cut his eye teeth in electoral politics before the 1918 General Election when he served as one of the guiding hands for Sinn Féin in a number of by-elections around the country. Those by-elections saw Count Plunkett, Éamon de Valera and jailed IRA man Joe McGuinness take seats against the candidates of an already terminally ill Irish Party. Indeed, the record shows that Collins was the driving force behind McGuinness and de Valera standing for election. In the case of McGuinness, Collins appears to have placed the man's name on the ballot without his approval. He ran McGuinness as the first imprisoned Sinn Féin candidate with the slogan, 'Put him in to get him out.'

Initially de Valera vehemently opposed the idea of members of the Volunteers, including himself, standing for election, largely on the basis that it would compromise their integrity as soldiers. De Valera, the only surviving leader of the Easter Rising, still saw himself principally as a soldier at this time. It was Collins who played a key role in changing de Valera's mind and who, ironically, in light of later events, was one of the catalysts for de Valera's almost seven decades in Irish political life.

The key tenet of Sinn Féin's electoral platform in the

by-elections during 1917–1918 and the 1918 General Election itself was its policy of abstention from Westminster. In the following, Collins describes the genesis of that policy as well as some of the early difficulties Sinn Féin faced as a disparate coalition and a burgeoning independence movement now taking on the mantle of party politics. In this we also get a glimpse of Collins, the political tactician. Perhaps even more important, we see his commitment to democratic politics that was evident years before the establishment of the Irish Free State.

When the first by-election after the Rising took place in North Roscommon in 1917, so much had the Republic of Easter Week been forgotten and so little had its teachings yet penetrated to the minds of the people that although the candidate was Count Plunkett whose son had been martyred after the Rising, he was returned only on the ground of his opposition to the Irish Party candidate.

Abstention from attendance at the British Parliament was the indispensable factor in the Republican ideal—the repudiation of foreign government. But it was only after his election that the Count declared his intention not to go to Westminster, and the announcement was not received enthusiastically by some of his most energetic supporters . . . This election and others which followed were not won on the policy of upholding a Republic, but on the challenge made to the old Irish Party. There was at this stage no unity of opinion on the policy of abstention among the various elements which formed the position which were joined together on [sic] to the Redmondites. As was known at the Plunkett Convention an effort was made to get all parts of the opposition united on such a policy, but the divergence of opinion was so great that to avoid a split it was declared that there should be no greater union than a loose cooperation.

At the South Longford election Joe McGuinness, who was then still in penal servitude, was elected on the cry, 'Put him in to get him out.' Abstentionism was put forward, but was so little upheld that he was returned with a majority of only 27. At the East Clare election, though, de Valera put forward the abstentionist policy and was elected by a large majority . . . and

56

at the three elections which followed in South Armagh, Waterford and East Tyrone the abstentionists were defeated. But the people were becoming educated and the union of the various sects and leagues in the big organisation of Sinn Féin . . . defined the national policy as abstentionist. The Republic of Easter Week had not lived on, as is supposed, supported afresh at each election, and endorsed finally in the General Election of 1918. But the people grew to put their trust in the new policy, and to believe that the men who stood for it would do their best for Ireland and, at the General Election of 1918, fought on the principle of self-determination, they put them in power.[1]

Collins played an even more significant role in Sinn Féin's campaign in the 1921 General Election, when Sinn Féin sought to revalidate the significant mandate it had won in 1918. It was to mark the first election since the enactment of the Government of Ireland Act (1920). We see in the following document how Collins's plans, running from the formation of election committees to the use of cars on polling day, give further testimony to his organisational prowess. They also inform the reader of the potential he held in a time of genuine peace for a democratic and independent Ireland. The first document, titled 'Directions about Cars for Polling Day', is a model of efficiency that would have been useful to any 'get out the vote' operation in a democratic society to this day. It also underlines Collins's practical qualities.

A car commander should be appointed at each polling station. He should see that the cars are properly distributed. He has the names of the townlands or streets arranged according to the roads by which they can best be worked. On the morning of the poll, he sends out an assistant to each central place in the district. As loads [voters] come in, he checks off the townlands or streets done, and sends out directions to his assistants.

The assistants get local men working on the different roads. They remain in a central place. They bring lists of voters in townlands or streets from which they work with local men. The local men collect loads each in his own district, and have them ready for the road when the car comes. Special care should be taken of invalids.

At each important crossroads it would be well to have men posted to give directions to drivers. All this means work, but REMEMBER [*sic*], a few votes missed in each townland or street might mean hundreds lost in the constituency. DON'T LOSE ONE [*sic*].[2]

A 'Revised Scheme for Elections' document drafted by Collins still stands as a thorough guide for the running of a constituency operation on election day. The topics included in the lengthy document covered: the duties of a constituency director; the duties of officer in charge of canvassing; bill posting and painting; literature; finance; transport; technical supervisor (legal); nomination papers; duties of volunteers in connection with elections; polling day instructions; and instructions for personating agents, among other headings. The section providing 'Instructions to Canvassers' is representative of the specificity and clarity of Collins's instructions.

See personally every voter on your list. Mark your list roughly beforehand showing political views of voters on whom you are about to call. Remember that courtesy often disarms opposition and that Sinn Féin desires to promote good will amongst all Irishmen. Impress on every voter the great importance of the issue in this election: whether Ireland is to become a free and independent nation or remain a subject province of the British Empire.

Every vote for Sinn Féin is a vote against conscription and this election will emphasise Ireland's case at the Peace Conference and ensure that our future freedom shall be guaranteed by the nations of the world. Study our leaflets in use in this election for facts and figures re taxation, conscription, and Ireland's ability to pay her own way and prosper as an independent state. . . . If a voter is doubtful, mark whether a second canvass would be advisable or not. If a voter be favourable, try to enlist his active support amongst his friends. If a car be wanted for election day, mark hour for calling . . . Where a voter is very ill mark whether a motor car be the best conveyance and if house is accessible by motor.[3]

As a candidate himself Collins cut an impressive figure. In all he stood for election on three occasions, 1918, 1921 and 1922. In the first two instances, he stood for two constituencies—one in his native Cork, the other for an Ulster constituency, a practice that was also followed by Éamon de Valera, among others, in elections for Dáil Éireann.

In hearing Collins's comment on elections before the War of Independence, we see that his belief in majority rule and the democratic process was already well formed. It did first evolve after the War of Independence and his efforts to establish the Irish Free State. In this respect Frank O'Connor's description of Collins as 'a conventional man who had been deprived of his conventions', is most useful.[4] His core values can be seen to be fairly straightforward. He believed in majority rule and the right of the Irish people to have self-determination, and in by-elections and in the 1918 General Election he fought for that right in the electoral process. When the will of the majority of the Irish people was denied and the parliament they elected—himself included—was driven underground, he took up arms against what he saw as unjust foreign rule, not unlike other young men in other nations in other times.

Our political machinery was altogether too efficient for the Irish Parliamentary Party organisation, and the election started by our having 25 unopposed returns. Many of the Sinn Féin candidates were men who were interned, and it must be admitted that the names of these candidates made an appeal in addition to the political appeal. It will be remembered that Sinn Féin immediately after the election sent representatives to London at the time of President Wilson's visit to lay a memorial [sic] of the Irish case before him.

Paralleling our political victories were the ever increasing acts of repression practised by the British Government, although at first neither England's aggression nor oppression were more than suggestions of what was to come. During the year England had pronounced Dáil Éireann, the Irish Republican Party, Sinn Féin, Cumann na mBan, the Gaelic League and the Gaelic Athletic Association illegal bodies. The civic courts were for the most part dispensed with and replaced by courts martial. For trivial offences severe sentences were inflicted. Possession of a card of membership in Sinn Féin earned a penalty of from six months to two years' imprisonment. Raids by armed bands of police and soldiers began to become frequent. Gradually it was becoming apparent that England had given up trying to rule Ireland with anything less than force.

The inevitable result of this policy—as indeed must have been anticipated by the British Government—was to drive the Irish people to meet desperate methods by desperate reprisals. The more extreme the British methods became, the more united our people grew.[5]

COLLINS IN DAIL ÉIREANN

In both the private and public sessions of Dáil Éireann, Michael Collins was a consummate performer. As Minister for Finance, other extenuating pressures on him notwithstanding, he showed himself in public debate to be well in command of his brief in addressing such questions as land annuities, the raising and administration of the Dáil Loan, etc. In, as we shall see, the separate section covering Collins's pronouncements on finance, he also used the floor of Dáil Éireann as a platform for criticising what he saw as counter-productive policies on a variety of fronts.

None the less, it would be disingenuous if we left the impression that Collins in the course of wearing his many hats in the Irish Revolution—including those at various times as Director of Organisation as well as Adjutant General of the IRA and its Director of Intelligence—was committed to an open discussion in full public view of the affairs of the Republic. He was well aware that the enemy was watching and he said as much by his virtual refusal to discuss military matters in the Dail in either private or public session.

COLLINS AND PARTITION

Despite having had little direct contact with north-east Ulster, although he was elected to a County Armagh constituency in addition to Cork in Dáil Éireann, Michael Collins evidenced a deep awareness of the damage he thought the British attempt to implement partition under the Government of Ireland Act 1920 would have on Ireland. An August 1921 memorandum to

Arthur Griffith, in which Collins seeks to analyse the impact of partition, is instructive both for showing how deeply he had thought about the topic and for the fact that, despite all his burdens in running the Department of Finance, directing the IRA's intelligence system, and helping lead the IRA, he still found time to strategise viewpoints. His comments at this time are also noteworthy in light of his future conduct during the Anglo-Irish negotiations and afterwards. The communication is also useful in that it underscores that partition was established in Ireland well before the Anglo-Irish Conference and the subsequent 1921 Treaty, and that Collins and Griffith as well as de Valera were fully aware of what the limits to any negotiations with the British were. The fact that partition already existed would make any attempt to use north-east Ulster as leverage in any negotiations with the British Government especially difficult.

> They [the Unionists within the Six County Northern Ireland jurisdiction] accepted it [partition] not as an expression of self-determination, but in order to prevent the wishes of the vast majority of their countrymen from being carried out: to use it as a means of preventing the real self-determination of Ireland . . . if the British Government says that such a Parliament must remain, it would indicate that it wishes to divide Ireland . . .

To Collins such a parliament would be a 'permanent danger to the future of the nation'. At the same time, he argued that an autonomous Northern Ireland parliament as part of a settlement that recognised Dublin as the capital of a single Irish jurisdiction and not Westminster was possible.

> There would be no such danger in Ireland herself granting local autonomy to a section of the population that expressed a clear and genuine wish for such autonomy . . . The Irish Government cannot recognise conditions illegitimately set up by the British Government, a government which has been repudiated by the Irish people and set up while the war was still in progress, and before terms of peace were discussed. When I read the Lloyd George offer, it seemed to me that it was not capable of being translated into a Treaty of Peace. Having made an offer to Ireland

he could not make it a condition that it should not apply to one-fifth of Ireland. His offer could be made to the 26 Counties and he could say that the status quo he had created in the Six Counties should remain intact.[6]

Yet within a year, while not embracing partition, Collins's views after the signing of the Anglo-Irish Treaty and the effort to gain public support for it in the 26 county jurisdiction it created in the South led him to make a leap of faith concerning British intentions in north-east Ulster that flew in the face of the views he expressed to Griffith. In a published essay in defence of the Treaty, he now had this to say about Irish unity.

Under the Treaty, Ireland is about to become a fully constituted nation. The whole of Ireland, as one nation, is to comprise the Free State, whose Parliament will have power to make laws for peace, order and good government of Ireland, with an executive responsible to that Parliament.[7]

What Collins's analysis neglected to mention, however, was that his was the theory behind the Treaty, at least as he saw it. Northern Ireland could still opt out of a unitary Irish state, which it did within hours of the Treaty's implementation. More evidence of what can best be described as Collins's wishful thinking relative to the North came in another exposition of his:

If they join in, the Six Counties will certainly have a generous measure of local autonomy . . . If they stay out, the decision of the Boundary Commission, arranged for in Clause 12 [Anglo-Irish Treaty] would be certain to deprive 'Ulster' of Fermanagh and Tyrone. . . . Shorn of these counties, she would shrink into insignificance. The burdens and financial restrictions of the Partition Act will remain on north-east Ulster if she decides to stay out. No lightening of these burdens can be effected by the English Parliament without the consent of Ireland. Thus union is certain. The only question for north-east Ulster is 'How soon?'[8]

At the same time Collins continued to be keenly aware of the harm partition presented from a nationalist perspective, while outlining the view that Britain intended to leave Northern Ireland sooner rather than later.

North-east Ulster had been created and maintained not for her own advantage, but to uphold Britain's policy . . . Everything was done to divide the Irish people and to keep them apart . . . She petted a minority into becoming her agents with the double advantage of maintaining her policy and keeping us divided. If we were kept in subjection we must be kept apart. . . . With the British gone the Orangeman loses that support which alone made him strong enough to keep his position of domination and isolation. Without British support he becomes what he is, one of a minority in the Irish nation. His rights are the same as those of every other Irishman, but he has no rights other than those.[9]

THE NORTHERN STATE: A PRIVATE WAR

Despite having to contend as Chairman of the Provisional Government with what Kevin O'Higgins termed the 'wild men' among their former colleagues in arms who threatened to overthrow the fledging Irish state, from March until August 1922 Collins was also involved in a war on another front. He sought earnestly to alter the second-class treatment meted out to Catholics in Northern Ireland. He was involved in a three-way confrontation involving Britain on the one hand—and Winston Churchill in particular—and the Northern regime itself left by Sir James Craig.

In the spring and summer of 1922 Northern Ireland and the treatment of the nationalist population in those six counties occupied much of Collins's thinking, even after the Civil War had got under way in earnest in the South at the end of June. As mentioned elsewhere in this effort, it was also a time of great personal stress for Michael Collins. His dilemma included the fissures that had developed by June 1922 between himself and his colleagues in the Provisional Government in relation to the Provisional Government's posture towards Northern Ireland.

Collins's active interest in north-east Ulster might also have been tied to an early realisation that the partition of Ireland and the existence of a separate Northern Ireland state had become more of a reality than he bargained for, promises from Lloyd George, among others, made to him in London notwithstanding. This understanding, before the Boundary Commission ever met, may have produced what appears at times an almost frantic effort to protect Catholics in some of the most vulnerable areas of the North from pogroms by loyalist mobs. Indeed pogroms did take place while Sir James Craig and Northern Ireland's military adviser and Collins's old adversary General Sir Henry Wilson did virtually nothing to stop them. [Wilson's assassination outside his home in London in June 1921 by members of the IRA appears to have been done on the orders of Collins, even as he led the Provisional Government. His sending of Liam Cullen to London in early July, in an attempt to free the two IRA men arrested for Wilson's slaying, certainly suggests some degree of culpability. If nothing else, it underscores the virtual double life he was leading at this time.] For its part, the British Government did little outwardly to even foster an appearance of evenhandedness, bringing little pressure to bear on Craig's regime in so far as the Catholic population was concerned. The exchanges between Collins and British leaders concerning Northern Ireland grew in their vituperation. They also give further testimony to Collins's passion and perhaps also a sense of guilt that he was unable to do more to protect the Northern nationalists who had become cut off from the rest of the Irish nation and who were now for all intents and purposes without a state.

In the final days of June 1922, during what must have been a period of extreme difficulty for Collins as he fought off the threat from Rory O'Connor and other opponents of the Treaty in the Four Courts under pressure from the British Government to act, he also found himself confronting that same British Government over what were for him disturbing developments in the North. On 28 June he protested vigorously to Winston Churchill against the Craig regime's decision to abolish the system of proportional representation for local government elections, thereby giving the nationalist population even less of a voice in the affairs of Northern Ireland.

The grave effect of this Bill on nationalist thought in Ulster and in general all over the country, coupled with Sir James Craig's attitude on the Boundary Commission, cannot be exaggerated.

Safeguards for the minority in our jurisdiction have frequently been demanded and readily granted by us. Our people in the

North are not slow to notice this, and continually put up to us that their rights under the Craig regime are not protected in the slightest degree. The introduction of this reactionary Bill has greatly strengthened this standpoint, and in consequence considerably weakened our influence. The effect of this enactment will be to wipe out completely all effective representation of Catholic and Nationalist interests. The Nationalist strongholds of County Fermanagh, County Tyrone, Derry City, as well as several urban and rural districts, will go and completely anti-Catholic juntas will reign in their place. You will agree, I am sure, that nothing could be more detrimental to the cause of peace.[10]

Indeed, when placed against the backdrop of more than a quarter-century of violent upheaval in Northern Ireland since 1969, Collins's analysis from 1922 of the shortcomings of the Northern state and Britain's failure to take adequate action during its formative stages to protect the democratic rights of the Catholic minority there can only be seen as prescient.

But Collins received little in the way of a positive assurance from Churchill. The course of events suggested that British policy in Northern Ireland was moving in the opposite direction: the full imposition of partition. On 9 August, the day before Arthur Griffith's death, Collins returned to the Craig regime effort to impose gerrymandering as the law in Northern Ireland.

Do you not see, or have His Majesty's advisers not disclosed, the true meaning of all this? Not merely is it intended to oust the Catholic and National people of the Six Counties from their rightful share in local administration, but it is, beyond all question, intended to paint the Counties of Tyrone and Fermanagh with a deep Orange tint in anticipation of the 'Ulster Month' and the Boundary Commission, and in doing so to try to defraud these people of the benefits of the Treaty.[11]

COLLINS: THE TREATY, FREE STATE AND CIVIL WAR

'What have we come for? I ask myself that question a dozen times a day.'
(Michael Collins to John O'Kane, October 1921)

It can be said with certainty that without Michael Collins there would not have been an Anglo-Irish Treaty concluded by the end of 1921. As we have seen, the considerable weight that Collins carried within the Irish Republican Army made his inclusion on any Irish negotiating panel sent to London vital if an agreement was to be struck that would appeal to those who waged conflict against the Crown in the highways and byways of Ireland during the years 1919 to 1921.

Herein, we will be hearing from Collins over the period of months spanning October 1921 to his death in August 1922. This period covers the negotiations of the Anglo-Irish Treaty, his relationship with de Valera and others, the Dáil debates on the Treaty, Collins's subsequent leadership role in establishing the Irish Free State under the Treaty, and with that his simultaneous involvement in the Civil War which claimed his life.

In entering this phase in Collins's life, we have seen something of the transformation he underwent between December 1920, when he was among the republican 'hawks' who opposed a move towards a Truce at that time, and a year later when he was a principal signatory of the Anglo-Irish Treaty document. We have seen that human as well as political and military factors may well have weighed in the apparent shift in Collins's outlook. By the time the Anglo-Irish Truce took effect in July 1921, Collins, perhaps more than any other rebel leader in Ireland, had lived an underground existence. Throughout the thirty-one months of the Anglo-Irish War he rarely left the confines of Dublin, hardly ever slept in the same bed twice in a row, and while occasionally enjoying a chance to play with his friends' children while on the run, often bemoaned his own inability to settle down and have a family. We know that there were brief interludes with Kitty Kiernan, the woman he loved. But Collins was in danger of capture or worse during virtually all of this period.

The death of colleagues in the line of fire, some like Cork city's Lord Mayor, Tomás MacCurtain, murdered in cold blood, had a profound effect on him. 'I have not much heart', he wrote to Terence MacSwiney following MacCurtain's death, 'in what I am doing today, thinking of poor Tomás. It is surely the most appalling thing that was done yet.'[1]

As a practical matter, the Anglo-Irish Truce probably provided the British Government with an important window from which to view Sinn Féin and the IRA. In essence they were flushed out into the open, a fact which Collins, as we have seen, conceded in private. It was also a fact which may have had a direct bearing on his private and public actions.

The Anglo-Irish Conference held in London from 11 October to 6 December 1921 provides an important vehicle for measuring the evolution that occurred in Collins's thinking as to the best course to be followed for a resolution of the conflict in Ireland's favour. Collins served effectively as chairman of the Irish delegation with Arthur Griffith. It was a development which may have also played a role in the Corkman's metamorphosis from IRA hard-liner to a practical nationalist willing to consolidate the gains that the Irish Revolution had achieved. This was due perhaps both to Griffith's predilection towards moderation and the respect Collins held for him. Clearly Collins's actions during the course of the eleven week-long Anglo-Irish Conference and its aftermath had a direct bearing on his and Ireland's future. The decisions made then have also of course contributed to defining Anglo-Irish relations right up to the present day.

The selection of Collins for the Irish delegation that went to London in October 1921, and de Valera's refusal to go, marked a role reversal from the latter's talks with Lloyd George in London the previous July. It is important to emphasise that what brought de Valera to London in July 1921 to meet Lloyd George directly and Collins and the Irish delegation to meet the British side the following October was the British invitation that they meet 'to ascertain how the association of Ireland with the community of nations known as the British Empire may best be reconciled with Irish national aspirations'. It was this phrasing which would encompass the interaction between the two countries from July to December of that year and which would impact directly on the internal debate between the Irish themselves thereafter.

In July 1921, as we have seen, de Valera went to England with a delegation that did not include Collins. In England, de Valera met the British Prime Minister alone during the course of several meetings spanning a week, but no satisfactory result was reached by either party. Why de Valera, three months later, sent Collins along with Griffith to head up the Irish delegation in the Anglo-Irish Conference is still a matter for conjecture.[2] The advice given de Valera by Harry Boland for sending Collins to London may have been a deciding factor. 'At the present time', he told de Valera, 'from what I have learned since I came back from America, you will not succeed in overthrowing the British militarily. If it's a question between peace and war, I'm for peace. If there are negotiations, I think Mick should go and I'll tell you why—in my opinion, a "gunman" will screw better terms out of them than an ordinary politician.' (The fact that Boland was still at this time locked in a fierce battle with Collins for the heart of one Kitty Kiernan may have had a little to do with his desire to see Collins sent to do what appeared to be the impossible in England.)

In the end Collins agreed to serve with Arthur Griffith as co-leader of the Irish delegation. In fact he was ordered to go. But at the outset of the Cabinet's effort to press him into service in what was for him the new role of negotiator, Collins argued that his best contribution lay in his staying at home, remaining the enigmatic IRA hard man to the British, whom de Valera could use as a counterweight to any British offer made. It was an advantage that Collins would lose from the moment he first walked into 10 Downing Street and he knew it. Collins told a private session of the Dail on 14 September 1921 after his appointment was made clear:

> To me the task is a loathsome one. I go, I go in the spirit of a soldier who acts against his best judgment at the order of his superior.[3]

Later he was more explicit about his feelings at a meeting with those who were perhaps his true soul mates, the IRB's executive.

> I have been sent to London to do a thing which those who sent me know had to be done but had not the courage to do it themselves. We had not, when these terms were offered, an average of one round of ammunition for each weapon we had. The fighting area in Cork . . . was becoming daily more circumscribed and they could not have carried on much longer.[4]

The fact that he might be made a scapegoat by rivals in the Cabinet was raised by some of his devotees within the IRB. But Collins accepted the risk once the decision to send him was made.

> Let them make a scapegoat or anything they will of me. We have accepted the situation as it is and someone must go.[5]

The Irish delegation brought with them to London on 11 October a set of counter-proposals to the terms offered by Lloyd George to Éamon de Valera on 20 July 1921. In sum, their proposals came under the headings of trade, finance, defence, the future of Ulster, and Ireland's relationship to the Crown and the British Empire as a whole. But it was the latter two topics that evoked the widest disagreement between the parties, as it would in the end with the Irish themselves. From the Irish delegation's standpoint, the negotiations centred on whether Ireland was to be a British dominion or an externally associated republic. Clearly, a necessary corollary to an association with the Crown would involve an oath of allegiance to it. The working of such an oath would be determined by the extent to which Ireland was affiliated with the Empire. Thus, de Valera's plan for external association, known as Document No. 2 and drafted by Erskine Childers—who would serve as the

Irish delegation's secretary—became the optimum Irish objective in London since it provided for the loosest possible form of allegiance to the Crown. But what was in de Valera's heart of hearts on that question, and what was in fact possible for Collins, Griffith and the others on the Irish side to achieve, were entirely different matters.

From the British standpoint, their effort was concentrated on delaying the raising of the issue of partition and north-east Ulster until the question of Ireland's status within the Empire and the role of the Crown in Irish affairs was resolved. But this decision may have been made more out of a practical grasp of the inherent ability of the Ulster question to derail an Irish settlement than out of some deep-rooted desire to ensure a divided Ireland. In a memorandum at the outset of the talks Lionel Curtis, the British legal adviser, cautioned Lloyd George that the government should avoid any appearance of equivocation by stating that while 'offering Dominion status it refuses to recognise the independence of Ireland'.[6]

For the first two weeks the Irish delegation developed a sense of accomplishment as it pressed its proposals at No. 10 Downing Street without any outward demonstration of British hostility. But by the end of October the major areas of disagreement had come to the fore at the Conference. The Irish proposals in relation to the Crown and Empire were given short shrift, with Lloyd George rejecting the idea of 'External Association' outright. It was here that Collins and Griffith set about obtaining the best terms possible. It became apparent that they and the rest of the delegation, while postponing agreement as to the exact form of words concerning the Crown's role as head of an association between Ireland and Britain, had offered a tacit willingness to accept partnership within the British Commonwealth.

By 25 October 1921, two weeks into the negotiations in London, Éamon de Valera became so alarmed, when he found out that Collins and Griffith were conducting meetings with Lloyd George and Austen Chamberlain apart from the rest of the Irish delegation, that he suggested joining them in London immediately. Of particular concern was Griffith's suggestion to de Valera that he appeared willing to accept a tacit recognition of the Crown in exchange for British recognition of Ireland's 'essential unity'. 'External Association' lay at the heart of de Valera's maximum position for any agreement on involvement with the British Empire. To him, acceptance of the Crown was contrary to that position. The following day Collins and Griffith wrote a reply which was signed by every member of the Irish delegation, taking umbrage at de Valera's suggestion. They made it clear that they saw his involvement as an infringement on their powers as plenipotentiaries as conferred on them by the Dáil.

> The delegates regard the first paragraph of your letter . . . as tying their hands . . . and as inconsistent with the powers given them on their appointment and numbers 1 and 2 of 'instructions to the Plenipotentiaries from the Cabinet' dated 7th of October. . . . Obviously any form of association necessitates discussion of recognition in some form or other of the head of the Association. Instruction No. 2 conferred this power of discussion but required before a decision was made reference to the members of the Cabinet in Dublin. The powers were given by the Cabinet as a whole. Having regard to the stage discussions have reached now, it is obvious that we could not continue any longer in conference and [will] return to Dublin immediately if this, however, is withdrawn. . . . we strongly resent, in the position we are placed, the interference with our powers. The responsibility, if this interference breaks the very slight possibility there is of settlement, will not and must not rest on the plenipotentiaries . . . As to your coming to London, we think, if you can come without it being known, it is important that you do so immediately. But if you cannot come privately, do not come publicly, unless we send you a message that in our opinion it is essential.[7]

De Valera, taken aback by the virulence of the Irish delegation's response, replied on 27 October that there was 'obviously a misunderstanding'. 'There can be no question', he wrote, 'of tying the hands of the plenipotentiaries beyond the extent to which they are tied by their original instructions.' It was to prove a fateful yet vague communication since it was unclear whether he was referring to the Cabinet's instructions or the set of contradictory ones he had subsequently issued to the delegation himself. He also dropped any further suggestion of going to London.[8] Clearly, throughout his time in London, Collins deeply resented what he saw as the unrealistic expectations of those, including de Valera, who remained behind in Dublin. At the same time he continued to harbour respect for Cathal Brugha, the latter's open hostility to him notwithstanding.

> We [Griffith and Collins] came to the topic for the thousandth time of the Dublinites. I have often said that Brugha commanded respect and I still say the same. I respect a fighter and B [Brugha] is one. Only he is misguided. Yet even in enmity he is capable of great sincerity—which is more than I can say of the others.[9]

A document written by Collins under a Dáil Éireann letterhead and submitted to the British Government in November 1922 during the Anglo-Irish Conference provides an important insight into how Collins's thought processes had evolved at this stage from that of a guerrilla warfare tactician and even brilliant financial organiser for a revolutionary government. The document was attached to the proposals for External Association which the Irish delegation had submitted to the Conference on 28 November. We see a return to the theme he had actually referred to in his boyhood essay written at Clonakilty National School when he spoke of a 'federation' of nations.

Collins's proposal appears to have been the result of much reflection on the topic. In it he outlined a view of how the British Commonwealth could evolve into a wider international organisation, one in which Ireland could play a role and indeed in which a creative Anglo-Irish agreement could serve as a catalyst. Students of British Commonwealth history would be well advised to compare the ideas outlined by Collins at this point to the British Cabinet with the language of the Statute of Westminster (1930) which would serve as the governing instrument for the Commonwealth. Such a comparison will underscore how British draftsmen eight years later had liberally borrowed from the ideas expressed by the same Michael Collins who had served as such a stalwart enemy of the Empire. His submission was titled 'On the Wider International Aspects of an Anglo-Irish settlement'. In it Collins theorised how the United States, apparently above and apart from its refusal to join the League of Nations, might be persuaded to join such an association comprised primarily it seems of English-speaking peoples. Collins's proposal began with a historical overview in which he enumerated instances of Britain's misgovernment of Ireland through the course of centuries. In his comments on the Great Famine of the nineteenth century, he stated outright his view: 'Half a million or more people were murdered by the British.' He then turned to what was possible between the two countries if sufficient good will was shown.

A new era is dawning, not only for Ireland, but for the whole world. The problem of associating autonomous communities can only be solved by recognising the complete independence of the several countries associated. Into such a league might not America be easy to enter?[10]

Drawing from his analysis of the Anglo-Irish Conference to date, he then offered the following:

British people do not recognise the change which has come about not only for Ireland and England but for the whole world. So that:
1. The business of the Irish Conference is to form some sort of alliance in which both may be associated for equal benefit.
2. The position of Ireland is entirely different from that of the British colonies.
3. Nevertheless, both England and Ireland, by nature of their nearness to each other, have matters of common concern.
4. The only association which will be satisfactory to Ireland to enter will be based not on the present technical legal status of the dominions, but on the real position they claim and have secured.
A development such as this might lead to a World League of Nations. From conflict (world conflict) to harmony.
If America were able to enter such a league, a further move would be made towards world peace. Consequently, in such an atmosphere—through improved relationship—to a condition of financial stability.
The invitation to the Irish representatives to consider how association with the nations of the British Commonwealth can best be reconciled with Irish national aspirations, makes it necessary to consider how far the members of the group have attained independent nationality. What steps should be taken to secure such a standard of independence.[11]

We see therein how the ideas of the idealistic young boy in west Cork, motivated by a concern for world peace, had developed into a proposal for the creation of an international organisation of nations less than two decades later as a specific proposal submitted to the rulers of the British Empire. Indeed, it might be said that we see in this initiative evidence of Collins returning to what he might have become in a more peaceful setting had war and revolution not interrupted his life. Submitted one month into the Anglo-Irish negotiations, it also revealed that while offering the Irish proposals for External Association as instructed by Dublin, Collins held a view that if dominion status was the most Ireland would be offered by Britain, then he would do his utmost to maximise the boundaries of that offer.

There was also other evidence from the Anglo-Irish Conference of Collins's capacity as a thinker. The head-to-head discussions between the Irish and British delegations at No. 10 Downing Street demonstrate Collins's ability as a debater when placed up against British officials of the calibre of Lloyd George, Winston Churchill and Lord Birkenhead, among others. The notes of Erskine Childers, taken for the Irish side, of an exchange that occurred between the parties on 14 October 1921 on the question of Ulster, which featured Collins and Griffith, is especially illustrative.

Arthur Griffith: If you don't throw your force behind Ulster we can agree. Six counties are not Ulster. Tyrone and Fermanagh — little to do with Antrim and Down . . . Donegal, most northern part of Ireland. It is in Southern Ireland . . . division unnatural. Ulster never eager for partition. They took land reform when we got it . . . [It is] as if six of your counties split off. You wouldn't stand it.

Lloyd George: I disagree. Wales in south-east, predominantly English—was once hostile. We said let them go. Left them to decide. They chose Wales. It is because we left them the choice. Cardiff ran 10 to 1 in favour of association with Wales.

Michael Collins: Wales is no analogy. North faced with coercion of a third of area. Belfast will be like Vienna . . .

Arthur Griffith: Supposing Germany took England and partitioned Yorkshire . . .

Lloyd George: We have to deal with the facts as well as justice.

We had [Home Rule crisis] to ask England to force Ulster out of a combination into another which she abhorred. Impossible. Shoot them down? . . . You say Ulster is our creation. Untrue. I tried in the war to bring Ulster in. Useless. Mistake to assume Ulster is opposed to partition. Glad to see you agree force is no use. Would draw into vortex . . . Ireland a desolation. What alternative?

Arthur Griffith: Withdraw.

Lloyd George: We propose to do it. Persuasion without pressure. We are not answering to divide Ireland . . .

Michael Collins: You are not standing aside. Unnatural boundaries. Prohibitions against disarming in 1913. Colonies no analogy. Administrative divisions only. [Collins's comments provoked shouts of 'No! No!' from the British side.] We cannot allow solid blocks to be coerced.

Lloyd George: Apply that to north Cavan . . . Deal with facts. Do not throw away opportunity.

Michael Collins: Different now. General wish to settle.[12]

The extent to which denial or a feeling of disbelief entered into Collins's attitudes towards the fact that the Northern Ireland Government, with its own parliament, prime minister and civil service was in operation as the Irish delegation sat in conference in London, is reflected in this exchange between Collins and Griffith with Lloyd George three days later.

Michael Collins: The Northern parliament is a joke.

Lloyd George: It will function tomorrow.

Arthur Griffith: It will never function. Our people will never consent to remain subject to it.[13]

There were also many lonely moments for Collins in London, especially as the negotiations deteriorated and he became increasingly alienated from de Valera and his Cabinet colleagues in Dublin and more incensed with the feeling that he and Griffith had been placed in an untenable position by de Valera. In a letter to his fiancée Kitty Kiernan on 15 November 1921, Collins described himself as feeling 'alone' and 'sad' while at the same time telling her he was prevented from writing a long letter because he was heading for a meeting with

Arthur Griffith and Lloyd George. Collins also mentioned that the British popular magazine, *Tatler*, which featured drawings of people in the news, had requested that he sit for them. 'What do you think of that now?' he asked.[14]

Compounding Collins's difficulties was his awareness that Lloyd George was by now doing his utmost to exploit the differences between himself, Griffith and others in the Irish delegation with their colleagues in Dublin. This knowledge on the British leader's part, Collins believed, was responsible for the uncompromising position the British side had taken on questions involving the Crown and north-east Ulster. Thus Collins told a friend:

> Not much achieved, principally because P.M. recognises our difficulty—Dublin.[15]

It was at this time, as Lloyd George prepared to face his own political difficulties and awaited the outcome of the Tory Party conference at Liverpool on 17 November, that Collins met with Griffith to assess where they stood. 'What will be the outcome if the present talks break down?' Collins pondered. The following are the possibilities he came up with:

> 1. A declaration of war by the British. 2. Cessation of hostilities on our part. We have mistakenly put all our cards on the table; we have laid ourselves open to the British. 3. Perhaps a continuation of efforts by the British to find a solution. This because world opinion is with us—providing that the British do not engage in full-scale war.[16]

In Griffith's view, at this stage a declaration of war by the British was unlikely. He believed that a return to the negotiating table was more likely. For Collins, the part of the dilemma the two of them faced also lay in Dublin.

> How best to reconcile our ideas with the fixed ideas at present held by certain members of the Cabinet? I will not agree to anything which threatens to plunge the people of Ireland into a war—not without their authority. Still less do I agree to being dictated to by those not embroiled in these negotiations . . . If they are not in agreement with the steps we are taking and hope to

take, why then did they themselves not consider their own presence here in London? Example, Brugha refused to be a member of the delegation.[17]

It is in the record of this meeting that we see Collins for the first time characterising an agreement with England that would provide Ireland with dominion status as a 'stepping stone' to fuller freedom—a full three weeks before he actually signed the Anglo-Irish Treaty. In addition, we see Griffith and Collins clearly weighing the outcome of their actions and at a minimum demonstrating a willingness to give the broadest possible interpretation to the authority given them by Dublin as plenipotentiaries.

> What are our powers? Are we to commit our country one way or the other, yet without authority to do so? . . . The advantages of dominion status to us, as a stepping stone to complete independence, are immeasurable.[18]

Collins also added this important caveat which is likely to have informed his subsequent actions. In his view, whether or not the British Parliament ratified the agreement, 'We are not committed until both the Dáil and Westminster ratify whatever agreement is made.'[19]

On 3 December a seven hour-long meeting with de Valera and the rest of the Cabinet in Dublin marked the last contact which Collins and Griffith had with their colleagues in Ireland prior to the signing of the Articles of Agreement three days later in London. At that session Collins was clear in some respects but vague in others as to what his views were. He argued that a rejection of the Treaty would be a gamble since Britain 'could arrange war in Ireland within a week'. And in an apparent contradiction of his earlier views on partition, he also stated that 'The sacrifice of north-east Ulster made for the sake of essential unity was justified.' But on the question of the oath to the Crown, he was still somewhat equivocal. He agreed that since the oath would not come into effect for one year from the signing of the agreement, he then questioned whether it would be worthwhile 'taking that twelve months' to see how the Treaty would work. He also suggested that the Dáil go to the country on the Treaty, but recommended 'non-acceptance' of the provision for the oath.[20]

Upon the delegation's return to London, a private meeting with Lloyd George proved pivotal in Collins's decision to sign the Treaty and accept the oath to the Crown as drafted by the British side. He did so largely on the basis of a commitment from the Prime Minister to let a 'Boundary Commission' allow the majority nationalist counties of Fermanagh and Tyrone withdraw from Northern Ireland if Sir James Craig refused to consent to Ireland's essential unity. A detailed memorandum which Collins prepared immediately after his meeting with Lloyd George underscores how the British assurances to him on Ulster had persuaded him to support the Treaty and to actively lobby for it. But in the absence of a British document confirming such an understanding, it still remains possible that Collins, determined to avoid a return to war, heard what he wanted to hear. In part his memorandum read:

> Mr Lloyd George remarked that I myself pointed out on a previous occasion that the North would be forced economically to come in. I said that the position was so serious, owing to certain recent happenings, that for my part I was anxious to secure a definite reply from Craig and his colleagues, and that I was agreeable to a reply rejecting or accepting. In view of the former we should save Tyrone and Fermanagh, parts of Derry, Armagh and Down by the Boundary Commission and thus such things as the raid in the Tyrone County Council and the ejection of staff. Mr Lloyd George expressed the view that this might be put to Craig.[21]

It was a weary yet reflective Collins who returned to the residence where the Irish delegation had been staying in London before dawn on the morning of 6 December 1921. The letter he composed to his friend John O'Kane almost immediately upon his arrival there, while his signing of the Agreement with the British was still most fresh in his mind, paints a compelling portrait of the burdens he had laboured under, and the growing pressures he would face upon his return to Ireland.

> When you have sweated, toiled, had mad dreams, hopeless nightmares, you find yourself in London's streets, cold and dank in the night air. Think—what have I got for Ireland? Something

which she has wanted these past seven hundred years. Will anyone be satisfied with the bargain? Will anyone? I tell you this —early this morning I signed my own death warrant. I thought at the time how odd, how ridiculous—a bullet might just as well have done the job five years ago.[22]

THE DÁIL DEBATES

The essence of Collins's position in Dáil Éireann in defence of the Treaty and his own actions in London drew on the wording of the invitation from Lloyd George which led the Irish delegation to London in the first instance. It is summed up in the following extract from the Dáil debates. It is a theme he would return to during debates and afterwards.

The communication of 29 September [1921] from Lloyd George made it clear that they were going into a conference not on the recognition of the Irish Republic . . . If we all stood on the recognition of the Irish Republic as a prelude to any conference we could very easily have said so, and that would have been it . . . it was the acceptance of the invitation that formed the compromise.[23]

For Collins what Ireland had gained under the Treaty from the standpoint of national rights was monumental.

England has renounced in fact all right to govern Ireland, and the withdrawal of their forces is the proof of this. With the evacuation secured by the Treaty has come the end to British rule in Ireland. The Treaty we brought home gave us the freedom we fought for, freedom from British interest and domination. The Black and Tans are no more. British military forces are gone, and these are the results of the Treaty, and we knew that December night, as we boarded the train for home, that these were the results of our many long months of arduous labours. It was a greater measure of success than any of us dared to hope.[24]

The issue of why he had in fact been sent to London in the first place by de Valera also gave rise to a lengthy tirade by Collins on the floor of the Dáil. While not detracting from the sense of duty that characterised his earlier comments about accepting in essence an order from his superiors, they none the less exhibit a sense of resentment on his part over the personal toll the process had exacted on his own personal popularity and also brought out into the open his resentment towards de Valera.

My going to London as one of the plenipotentiaries was in spite of my convictions that any other Irishman would serve the cause of Irish freedom better . . . For three hours one night, after the decision had been made to send a delegation to London, I pleaded with de Valera to leave me at home and let some other man take my place as a negotiator. But it was no use. My arguments seemed to fall on deaf ears; I had no choice; I had to go. Of course we all knew that, whatever the outcome of the negotiations, we could not hope to bring back all that Ireland wanted and deserved to have, and we, therefore, knew that more or less opprobrium would be the best reward we could hope to win.

But as Arthur Griffith has told you, we went when others refused to go, because it was a job that had to be done by somebody. For my own part I anticipated the loss of position I held in the hearts of the Irish people as a result of my share in what was bound to be an unsatisfactory bargain. And to have to hold the regard of one's fellow countrymen is surely a boon not to be lost while there is a way to hold it. But this consideration was not at all what moved me to try to keep out of the negotiations. Whether de Valera understood the advantage of keeping me in the background—whether he believed my presence in the delegation would be of greater value—or whether, for motives best known to himself, he wished to include me among the scapegoats who must inevitably fail to win complete success, is of little importance. The only fact that may appeal to the careful reader as significant is that before the negotiations began no doubt of de Valera's sincerity had a place in my mind.[25]

The contentiousness of Document No. 2 and whether Collins and Griffith had put up a sufficient fight for this proposal given them by de Valera and drafted by Childers pervaded much of the debate. For Collins it was a quibble over mere words, while to de Valera it meant the difference between freedom and the surrender of Irish sovereignty to the British monarch. In the Dáil's debates in private session Collins was adamant that what de Valera and his supporters were seeking by introducing Document 2 back into the fray again was a mere splitting of hairs that was simply not worth the price in terms of the turmoil back into which it would thrust the Irish nation. It was for this reason that he wanted a full debate in the Dáil's public session to underscore how slim the differences were between the Treaty he signed and the language of the oath as expressed in Document No. 2 that de Valera wanted.

> I want to give the interpretation of a man who has faith in Irish aspirations and who means to go before the Irish people of the Free State making our own precedents . . . not accepting the constitutional usage in Canada or any other place because all these things have advanced in the history of these nations and we have done a thing here under this Treaty . . . that has never been done in history. It is no longer the British Empire, it is the community of nations known as the British Empire. The British Empire always stood for domination. . . . In this Treaty it abandons this domination over Ireland. I want to go into all this not here but in the public session. I want to put it forward on that basis. I want to tear up Document No. 2 . . . and I want to show how we can work up our nationhood and freedom. . . . I have been at a disadvantage all the time until we go into public session. I want to appeal from the members of the Dáil to the general public which does understand these things in the plain Irish way that I understand them myself.[26]

During the debates de Valera also tried to offer another plan as an alternative to the Treaty. To Collins it was a further act of disingenuousness on de Valera's part.

> I am glad the President has given us this proposal. We put this proposal. In some ways I think some of the things we have secured from a verbal point of view are better. We put this before the other side with all the energy we could. That is the reason that I wanted certain vital documents and these will show that the

same proposals that the President has now drafted have been put already. Let this thing be put up as what the Dáil agrees upon. That is what we are told here. But I for one want to have it on record that we have put up this already and that we have failed at it. There is no other delegation that would have got a better . . . treaty than the delegation that went.[27]

It was Collins's contention that the Treaty should be voted on its merits by the Dáil, up or down. He would accept the outcome, recognising that any future role would not be the same as the role he had previously played in the Irish struggle. He also argued that rejection of the Treaty would have left the role of any future Irish negotiating team most untenable.

If war is to follow I accept that decision, and whatever capacity my services can be of assistance.

. . . Let the Treaty be rejected and let those who take the responsibility for its rejection put that to the country . . . But let it be understood that no delegation should go back to these people whom we distrust. I know the answer they would get: 'You can go to the devil. You can't speak for anyone. You can't deliver the goods.' In my opinion they won't treat with any other delegation . . . We recommend the ratification of this document . . . If we cop this thing the British Parliament will chop it . . . Let there be no mistake about the alternatives. We have heard about the alternatives. We have heard about external and internal association. Association means association with them. . . . I would prefer to see the document rejected absolutely to passing these proposals, and having taken responsibility for that rejection it means that we are challenging them as a nation to a military decision. Well, I believe they are prepared to give belligerent rights if we made that decision. . . . I am standing not for shadows but for substance and that is why I am not a compromiser.

Collins continued to take umbrage at de Valera's attempt to resurrect Document No. 2.

We were not able to prevail upon them [the British] to accept it. Don't put us in the position of doing anything else than what we tried to do. If I went to Lloyd George he would say: 'If I accept this document [No. 2] you will come back after and say "We can't accept this now. I want my Republic." That would be in reality the position as I see it . . . The correspondence shows that we have already tried it. And I, as one man, can do no more.[28]

In the private sessions of Dáil Éireann covering the Treaty debates, we see a Michael Collins who is at once angry at the recriminating attacks he has received from those who were now rapidly becoming his adversaries, and also one determined to bring the debates back to full public session.

We are now on trial because we are not constitutional lawyers. Did anybody suggest I was a constitutional lawyer before I went over there? I saw some of our barristers and they looked damned poor fry before some of the other fellows. They didn't do as well as some of the fighting men did before them. How do I know what our lawyers are going to do without law? We noticed on the following day that this document didn't bear the words 'Treaty between Great Britain and Ireland'. We immediately arranged for this to be put in. If we are expected to be constitutional lawyers and to know how all free states in the world came into existence now is not the time to tell it.[29]

To the criticisms levelled against himself and Griffith for meeting with Lloyd George and Winston Churchill apart from the rest of the delegation, Collins was equally vociferous while repudiating outright the complaint raised by Robert Barton in repudiating his own signature to the Treaty that the delegation had signed the document 'under duress'.

It seems to me the point is not well taken. I have never heard anyone criticise de Valera for having conferred quite alone with Mr Lloyd George a few months earlier. There are inevitably details in the course of the negotiations of this character which are best discussed by a few men, rather than by dozens. And if, as Brugha charged, we were bungling amateurs, the fault lies with those who sent us . . . It has been charged that we signed the Treaty under duress. It has been said we signed under a threat of 'immediate and terrible war'. That is untrue. It was Barton who first made that charge and by his own statement proved himself a man who could be successfully threatened. But Barton challenged to quote the exact words used by any of the English plenipotentiaries . . . admitted that it had never been voiced in words.[30]

Just one week earlier, although the topic was still the Treaty, Collins portrayed a different side to one he loved dearly. To Kitty Kiernan, he wrote: 'I don't know how things will go now but with God's help we have brought peace to this land of ours —a peace which will end this old strife of ours for ever.' He was not to be the last Irishman to have made such a claim, albeit for the most genuine of reasons.[31] The space of little more than a week yielded little peace of mind for Collins. As the Dáil debates on the Treaty headed towards a conclusion, he still had a sense of foreboding that this would by no means mark the end of the internal quarrel.

Am up early this morning, and am not feeling well at all unfortunately. The times are getting worse indeed and these coming days will be worse still, but I suppose they'll be over and done with soon enough.[32]

A careful review of the Dáil debates will not reveal questions involving Northern Ireland and partition, either in the public or private sessions, as significant features of the Treaty debates. None the less, the issues loomed in the background. They were related to the central issue debated: the oath to the Crown and the relationship of Ireland to the British Empire. While Collins's views on partition and Northern Ireland are covered in greater detail subsequently, it is here, within the context of the lengthy debate of 19 December 1921 that his defence of the Boundary Commission provision in the Treaty belongs. In his remarks we also see that the policy of the 'non-coercion' of north-east Ulster is the one he clearly supports.

We have stated we would not coerce the north-east. We have stated it officially in our correspondence, stated it publicly in Armagh and nobody has found fault with it. What did we mean? Did we mean we were going to coerce them? What was the use of talking big phrases about not agreeing to the partition of the country? Surely we recognise the north-east corner does exist, and surely our intention was that we should take such steps as would sooner or later lead to mutual understanding. The Treaty has made an effort to deal with it, and has made an effort, in my opinion, to deal with it on lines that will lead very rapidly to goodwill and the entry of the north-east under the Irish Parliament. I don't say it is an ideal arrangement, but if our policy is, as has been stated, a policy of non-coercion, then let somebody else get a better way out of it.[33]

Perhaps the most poignant insight into Collins's feelings, the respect he still held for those he toiled with both dead and alive for Ireland's freedom, and the degree to which he had developed as a democrat, were made especially evident prior to the adjournment of the Dáil debates on the Treaty at Christmas 1921.

Deputies have spoken about whether dead men would approve of it [the Treaty], and they have spoken whether children yet unborn would approve it, but few have spoken of whether the living approve of it. In my own small way I tried to have before my mind what the whole lot of them would think of it . . . There is no one here who has more regard for the dead men than I have. . . . I think the decision ought to be a clear decision on . . . the Treaty as it is before us . . . Don't let us put the responsibility, the individual responsibility, upon anybody else. Let us take that responsibility ourselves and let us in God's name abide by that decision.[34]

DEFENDING THE NEW IRISH STATE

The Dáil's ratification of the Treaty by a margin of seven votes by no means ended the division over the Anglo-Irish Treaty. Although defeated in the Dáil, de Valera and his supporters set out almost immediately to make the implementation of the Treaty untenable. To Michael Collins fell the brunt of the effort to build public support among the ordinary Irish people not only for the Treaty but for the creation of the Provisional Government that would oversee the transition into the Free State. He did so from the public platform throughout much of

Ireland during the period January to April 1922. In short order he became Chairman of the Provisional Government, the temporary entity created to facilitate the transition to the Free State, while Griffith replaced de Valera as President of Dáil Éireann in January 1922. In effect Southern Ireland had two governing bodies, while the Northern Ireland state was already in existence by this time, with Sir James Craig already ensconced as its Prime Minister in his 'Protestant state for a Protestant people'. The following extract from an address Collins made at a public meeting held in Dublin on 5 March 1922 provides an insight both into his powers of persuasion and evidence of his resentment towards those who he believed sought to thwart the will of the people.

Mr de Valera's campaign is spoken of as a campaign against the Treaty. No it is not a campaign against the Treaty . . . but a campaign against the Free State. And not only against the Free State but still more against those who stand with the Free State. They [de Valera's supporters] say 'We stand against the Treaty and for the maintenance of the Republic.' That is very curious. Because we were told by a member of the Dáil Cabinet that before the Truce of July last it has become plain that it is physically impossible to secure Ireland's ideal of a completely isolated Republic in the immediate future otherwise than by driving the overwhelmingly superior British forces out of the country. The Republic was an ideal which it was physically impossible to secure last July. By February [1922] it has become their policy to maintain the Republic. In his speech at Ennis last Sunday, Mr de Valera repeated that he was not a doctrinaire republican. He said it was a symbol, an expression of the democratic right of the people of Ireland, to rule themselves without interference from any outside power . . . I do not quarrel with that description. The Republic was a symbol, and an expression of our right to freedom.[35]

Collins went on to level charges of perfidy against de Valera and his supporters, while also emphasising to the public, as he had tried to explain earlier in the Dáil, the complexity of the situation in north-east Ulster. It should be noted that his views on partition and the setting up of Northern Ireland at this time represent an evolution from the attitudes he displayed on the same subjects in his remarks to Arthur Griffith the previous August.

We could not beat the British out by force so the Republican ideal was surrendered. But when we had beaten them out by the Treaty, the Republican ideal which was surrendered in July is restored. The objective of Mr de Valera and his party emerges. They are stealing our clothes. We have beaten the British by means of the Treaty. While damning the Treaty, and us with it, they are taking advantage of the evacuation which the Treaty secures. . . . In addition, we must remember there is a strong minority in our country up in the north-east that does not yet share our national views, but has to be reckoned with. In view of these things, I claim that we brought back the fullest measure of freedom obtainable—the solid substance of independence.[36]

On the public hustings we also see that Collins sought to empower his listeners and by so doing made it clear that it was their patriotic duty to uphold the Free State. He was explicit both in what he saw as the gains made by the Treaty and the damage that would be done if the fledgling Irish state was overthrown from within.

Have we betrayed you? I claim that we have got in the Treaty the strongest guarantee of freedom and security that we could have ever got on paper, the greatest amount of real practical freedom in the evacuation of their troops. In their place we have the right to have our own troops . . . The status which we accepted, which we forced the British to define, was the constitutional status of Canada. You destroy our hopes of national freedom, you will destroy all realisation in our generation of the democratic right of the people of Ireland to rule themselves without the intervention of a foreign power. . . . Britain is in a stronger position than she was in July. She has offered us and has agreed with us on a peace which the world considers a fair peace. In July world opinion was against her. World opinion is no longer against her.[37]

One week later, Collins issued similar sentiments as the principal speaker at a demonstration in support of the Treaty in

Cork city. Despite gunfire emanating from the crowd, Collins persisted with his speech. On this occasion Collins compared de Valera to a captain who had left his ship during troubled times.

And while the captain was away from his ship—that time in America—the weather was very stormy. There was a regular hurricane blowing—you in Cork will remember. The helm had been left by the captain in the hands of those same incompetent amateurs who afterwards in calm water had the ship on the rocks. And while he was away, somehow or other we steered it safely through those troubled waters . . . Mr de Valera laments, he says, that it should be necessary for him to remind the Irish people to be firm on the Republic. He had to ask those who were confusing the issue whether it was not a fact that the Republic was established by the Irish people? Why does Mr de Valera not answer his question? Well perhaps he cannot! It is not too easy when one has been confusing issues to make them clear again. But I will help him. What does Mr de Valera mean by a Republic? Fortunately he has told us in a speech he made last Sunday week in Ennis. He means by a Republic, he says, the democratic right of the people of Ireland to rule themselves without interference from any outside power. Accepting that definition I can answer Mr de Valera's questions. The Irish people have not disestablished their democratic right to rule themselves. They have claimed that right and fought for it through many generations. They have now at last established that right. They have done more. They have secured recognition of that right by the Power [sic] which through all the centuries had denied it. . . . If Mr de Valera's definition is right we could never have had a republic hereto. It was therefore never established because it is only now by means of the Treaty that the interference by the outside Power has ceased. That interference has come to an end . . . the absence of which Mr de Valera lays down as the condition necessary for the existence of a republic. We took a certain amount of government out of the hands of the enemy while he was here. We took as much as we could . . . But the enemy is going—will soon be gone, if, indeed, Mr de Valera and his friends will but allow him to depart.[38]

CIVIL WAR

No more than any other such travesty which pitted brother and sister against brother and sister, the Irish Civil War was not planned. The issues that provoked it were out in the open, and doubtless fuelled by inflammatory rhetoric. Over the course of the six months between January and June 1922, those who had fought together against British rule slid towards armed conflict against each other at a pace that contained its own terrible momentum.

The most graphic attack on the Provisional Government by Anti-Treatyite elements of the IRA came on 14 April 1922 when the Four Courts—the nerve centre of the legal establishment in Dublin—was seized. From the first day of its occupation until Collins's decision to attack the buildings some ten weeks later, a position of stalemate existed with neither wishing to fire the first shot. For the Anti-Treatyites under Rory O'Connor the objective was to provoke a British return and a British attack upon the Four Courts garrison. But this was anathema to Collins who viewed this as undermining one of the principal accomplishments of the Treaty: the evacuation of the British Army from most of Ireland.

None the less it appears that O'Connor and Collins, along with others on both sides of the Treaty divide, hoped that the IRA could be reunited by a joint enterprise aimed at making the Northern Ireland state untenable. But even for the most machiavellian of creatures, events conspired to make such a plan unworkable. In the end under the orders of Michael Collins the Four Courts garrison was attacked during the early hours of 28 June. But he waited until virtually every other avenue was tried before he gave the order to attack. Collins genuinely did not want to accept that those inside the Four Courts had become his former comrades. He wanted to avert causing death or injury to those with whom he served in the Irish struggle, and indeed to avoid casualties on all sides. He also hoped against hope that reason would prevail. He also fully grasped the horror which a civil war represented and when he blurted out in a fit of pique that Churchill should 'do his own dirty work', he meant it. Collins must also have sensed that the sight of Irishmen fighting Irishmen would have caused little grief for the British Government. Above all, a civil war would

destroy his hopes of using the Treaty to build the fuller freedom
he had spoken of so often.

But when his decision to attack the Four Courts finally
came, Collins acted out of the more pressing concern that if he
didn't act decisively the British Army would return to Ireland.
And for him, among the most practical of men, this represented
both a short and long-term disaster for Ireland as a whole.

By the end of June the Free State Army was in a stronger
position in Dublin. Collins also had the advantage of having the
June elections behind him and a clear-cut mandate in his view
from the Irish people to act on their behalf in defence of the
Treaty. Thus it was at 4 a.m. on 28 June that the Free State
Army under Collins's orders commenced the bombardment of
the Four Courts. It was without doubt one of the most
distasteful decisions he would ever have to make. The attack
also marked the end of the cooperation between the Anti-
Treatyites and elements within the Free State to destabilise the
Northern state.[39] But the initial Free State bombardment was
not sufficient to bring about the surrender of the republicans.
Collins was forced to seek further assistance from the British.
A request from Collins to General Macready for more shells for
the 18 pound guns was turned down. This led Collins to
telephone Churchill and the latter set in motion the transfer of
300 more shells from the British arsenal. On 30 June the Four
Courts fell. In a statement released on the day the
bombardment commenced, Collins sought to explain that the
reason for his action was to 'secure the people of Ireland against
further molestation and interference with their liberties'. The
kidnapping on the streets of Dublin of Free State General
'Ginger' O'Connell by Anti-Treatyite forces a few days earlier
became Collins's principal public *raison d'être* for action.

On Saturday last two Dublin firms received demands in the
names of persons in the Four Courts to pay certain sums of
money by the following Tuesday. The demands were put forward
under the pretext of the Belfast boycott, which has no authorised
existence. The Provisional Government on receiving information
of the attempted extortion arranged to have the persons
attempting it arrested if and when they proceeded to enforce their
demand. Forty-eight hours later information received by the
Government that a raid was being carried out by similar persons

on the premises of Messrs Ferguson, Baggot Street. Orders were immediately issued to the troops to protect the firm. This order was carried out and the leader of the raiders was arrested and lodged in [*sic*]. This warning to the lawless and irresponsible that the Government, having received an emphatic mandate from the Irish people, would no longer tolerate any interference with their liberty and property was not heeded and insolently defied. Some hours later, the same evening, Lieut. Gen. O'Connell, Assistant Chief of Staff, while on his way through the streets alone and unarmed, was seized by an armed party of men and brought a prisoner to the Four Courts. The Provisional Government thereupon ordered the army to take action. This morning, the troops surrounded the Four Courts and demanded the evacuation of the building and the surrender of the munitions and property held therein. A time limit was given but the demand was ignored. At the same time the Fowler Hall which had been used as a centre of direction for the seizure of private property was invested.

Statements that British troops are cooperating with the IRA [*sic*] are false and malicious. None but the regular Irish forces— with the cooperation of the citizens who are loyally and enthusiastically supporting the Government—are engaged in putting down the disorderly elements who attempt to tyrannise over the people and defy their will.[40]

Collins reserved strong criticism for those who had served as his channels for importing arms into Ireland during the War of Independence and were now helping to arm the Anti-Treatyites against the Free State Army. At the same time, in chastising one such source, he also took the opportunity to emphasise why the Free State must be allowed to go forward as the best way for achieving an independent Ireland.

By this time you will have seen where our opponents have led the country and you must have seen that any 'stuff' you may be sending them is being used, or will most certainly be used, for shooting down our fellow countrymen. Believe me, the Treaty gives us the opportunity we may never get in our history for going forward to our ideal of a free independent Ireland. This cannot be gained without very much work yet — very hard work and perhaps more than hard work. And it is not by dissipation of the national energy that we can gain this. It is not by acts of suppression and it is not by denial of liberty that we can reach liberty.[41]

JULY–AUGUST 1922—THE END APPROACHES

In the final weeks of his life the portrait of Michael Collins that emerges is one of a deeply torn and troubled young leader trying to balance what were often competing agendas, military, civil and diplomatic in both the North and the South. By mid-July 1922 he had resigned as Chairman of the Provisional Government's Cabinet, ostensibly to concentrate on the prosecution of the Free State Army's efforts against the Irregulars. It bears reminding that at this time he was still only 31 years of age.

It is noteworthy that by the time Collins left the Cabinet in mid-July 1922, rifts had developed between himself and a number of his colleagues in the Provisional Government, most notably with Ernest Blythe. The Cabinet minutes show that a split had indeed emerged between the two men over the Free State's policy towards the Northern Ireland Government. Collins on a number of fronts sought to make the situation in the North for the Craig regime unworkable. And, as we will see, Collins's disagreement with the British Government and with Winston Churchill in particular over its treatment of the nationalist population in Northern Ireland had intensified by this time.

Collins had also become worn down by mental and physical stress. He had grown short tempered, and by mid-August, after assuming the leadership of the Irish Free State upon the sudden death of Arthur Griffith, he was suffering from walking pneumonia. But he was unable to take the necessary bed rest.

Despite his burdens, Collins continued to make time for visits from journalists and prominent figures from abroad. The impression left by Collins on one visitor, US Senator James D. Phelan of California, on the morning of 31 July 1922, is published herein for the first time. It is useful in conveying the purposefulness of Collins's outlook during this very difficult period for Ireland. At the same time there is a certain wistfulness in Collins's replies to the questions put to him by Senator Phelan.

General Collins, who appeared in uniform, is a handsome heavy-set youth. He has all the charm of boyishness and much of its shyness, and gives an impression of that combination of gentleness and strength that is probably characteristic of all potentially great leaders. His smile is most engaging . . . and though his eyes are frequently cast down he gives no suggestion of furtiveness or a lack of frankness. When he speaks, one is more conscious of fluency than eloquence.

Referring to the Treaty he expressed himself as believing that Ireland had received more through it than he or many of his associates had hoped for. The word 'Republic' had been made use of, practically with the general expectation that at least dominion rule would result, and under the Treaty Ireland had obtained more than this. The advantage the Treaty offered could serve as a means to an end which some day would be complete separation. The dismemberment of the British Empire is imminent if not already begun. It need not necessarily come through war or revolution. For the moment, it was admissible for England to allow a potentially hostile state to come into existence, far less to consent to becoming the author of its being; and Ireland herself was in position to assume responsibility of, for instance, the naval protection of her coasts which complete separation from Britain would have necessitated. England's generosity was not spontaneous or naive, of course. Her remembrance of 1916 and pressure from the United States and the outside world are responsible for the terms of the Treaty.

General Collins would make no prediction as to Ireland's immediate future, nor did he promise that Dublin had seen the end of her troubles as he had hoped when the Four Courts was destroyed. Cork, he admitted, was now the goal of the Free State troops and the people there are all sympathetic to them. When asked if they would not resent the shelling of their city for the second time, the General made some reference to the heartlessness of matches, powder and petrol which knew neither remorse nor regret. He mentioned also that one of his best friends was in command of the Irregular troops [Liam Lynch], said to be about two thousand strong, massed in Cork at the present time. . . . the mention of Mr de Valera's name called forth no comment from General Collins, who told of the attempted escape of Harry Boland which that morning had resulted in his being perhaps fatally wounded. When asked if there was any message he wished to send to the American people, Collins replied: 'Give them our kind regards and say when all this is ended we'll come over and explain it to them.'[42]

Perhaps the most succinct explanation of all that Collins offered in retrospect for his support of the Treaty came in the following:

We took as much of the government of Ireland out of the hands of the enemy as we could, but we could not grasp all of it because he used the whole of his forces to prevent us doing so, and we were unable to beat him out of the country by force of arms. But neither had he beaten us. We made Ireland too uncomfortable for him. There were too many ambush positions in country areas, and too many gloomy street corners in Cork and Dublin. The British had not surrendered and had no need to agree to a settlement that would secure for us their withdrawal and evacuation. There were humiliating terms for a settlement that would secure for us their withdrawal and evacuation. There was duress, of course. On their side, the pressure of world opinion to conform their practice to their professions, to make an honourable peace with us. On our side, the duress the weaker nation suffers against the stronger.[43]

As Collins's pressures grew, and his time on earth narrowed, the loss of old friends to the division provoked by the Treaty troubled him even more deeply. None was as painful as the split that developed between himself and Harry Boland. On 28 July 1922 Collins sent Boland a letter that was to mark the last contact between them. It also revealed the bitterness Collins felt at the obvious hold which de Valera had come to hold over Boland's loyalty.

Harry—It has come to this!
    Of all the things it has come to this. It is in my power to arrest you and destroy you. This I cannot do. If you will think over the influences which have dominated you it should change your ideal.

You are walking under false colours. If no words of mine will change your attitude, then you are beyond all hope—my hope.[44]

As we have seen, the two men had vied for the affections of Kitty Kiernan, with Collins emerging as the winner. How much this conspired to determine Boland's opposition to the Treaty and his subsequent antipathy to Collins we will never know. But we know that Collins and Kitty discussed Harry and the irrevocable parting of the ways between them, although it is evident that the young woman still maintained a friendship with Boland herself.

Only days after Collins's letter to him, Boland was shot at his home by members of the Free State Army. He would survive for one day, mortally wounded. Collins wrote to Kitty, noting the deep feelings of affection he continued to harbour for his fallen ex-comrade. He did so despite an awareness that Boland on his deathbed had expressed his hopes for Collins's own demise.

Last night I passed Vincent's Hospital and saw a small crowd outside. My mind went into him lying dead there and I thought of the times together, and, whatever good there is in any wish of mine, he certainly had it. Although the gap of eight or nine months was not forgotten—of course no one can ever forget it—I only thought of him with the friendship of the days of 1918 and 1919. They tell me that the last thing he said to his sister Kathleen, before he was operated on, was 'Have they got Mick Collins yet?' I don't believe it so far as I am concerned, and if he did say it, there is no necessity to believe it. I'd send a wreath but I suppose they'd return it torn up.[45]

But soon 'they' would get Mick Collins. Before leaving Dublin to complete a tour of inspection of the South that had been interrupted by the death of Arthur Griffith, Collins exclaimed: 'I'm going to try to bring the boys around. If not, I shall have to get rough with them.'[46]

In Cork city during that faithful last trip, Collins shooed away a nephew—a soldier in the Free State Army seeking to join his convoy—with this curt reply: 'I've got my job to do and you've got yours. Mind your own business and do your own work.' Later he stated to a collegue matter of factly, 'I believe

Dev's knocking around this area."[47]

An entry in his diary for 21 August 1922 noted the death of a young soldier at the hands of the Anti-Treatyites also named Michael Collins. The last entry in that diary would be made at 6.15 a.m. on 22 August 1922. In it Collins noted the towns he planned to visit that day: 'Macroom, Bandon, Clonakilty, Rosscarberry and Skibbereen.' Missing was a place he had possibly never heard of before, and which he likely still knew little of as he entered it at dusk on a warm summer evening, ironically for the second time that day. But Béal na Bláth was to become a place that Ireland would never forget.

7

COLLINS'S VISION FOR IRELAND

One of the most compelling yet wistful aspects of Collins's legacy is the vision he left for Ireland's economic and social development. A careful examination of the policies and ideas Collins advanced for an independent Ireland underscores perhaps better than any other aspect of his public statements, writings or letters, the scale of his vision for what Ireland could become and what he would have done to make the country's economic advancement possible.

A series of ideas for building public support behind what he saw as necessary economic development initiatives for the country, which Collins forwarded to Desmond FitzGerald on 12 July 1922, are particularly informative. In the document Collins outlined his ideas for the use of the cinema as a tool for winning public support for the nation-building that lay ahead. 'Great and quick results', he remarked, 'are bound to flow from there.' The use of film as a tool for public awareness, he noted, had been tried elsewhere 'with remarkable success . . . Since writing my last memo I hear that Germany has used very largely the cinema for these purposes.'[1] Collins had more in mind, however, than the use of the cinema for propaganda purposes. He sought to focus 'the people's minds on the great problems of construction and retrenchment'. He suggested the use of 'picturesque photos showing the broad seas, calm, wild, etc., with such captions as the "Atlantic gold-mine—full of wealth for the taking of it". By way of contrast, he proposed the use of other film segments

. . . showing the poor, ill equipped little fleets of the poor people. . . . This section will show the reason they are so poor and go as harvesters to England and Scotland. Show them the well-equipped up-to-date trawlers of Great Britain which poach on them. [Then say] Fellow countrymen, this is one of the problems. It rests with us now to equip these fishing folk and make them as prosperous as the English and the Scotch [sic]. To do this we must have peace and stable conditions in our country.[2]

Collins also sought to focus public attention upon other areas needing economic development. He suggested:

. . . photos showing the appalling distress in Connemara [sic], Donegal and other maritime counties . . . the awful little huts of the people—the Gaelic speaking people too—their poor dress, food, their barren fields, sowing corn growing among great boulders as I have seen in Donegal . . . Other pictures could show: 1. Our barren mountainsides as they should be [contrasted by photos of] Swiss mountainsides covered with areas of noble pines and other trees . . . [show] what Holland has done to save and reclaim her little land.[3]

He was also concerned about the plight of many of Ireland's urban dwellers, suggesting the use of films showing the terrible slums, the long ranks of unemployed, with counter-pictures of the 'garden suburbs they will have to be turned into'. Self-efficiency in energy and a focus on industrial development were also, quite remarkably, subjects addressed by Collins in his memorandum to FitzGerald—the father of a later Irish Prime Minister.

[For] the great question a national power generator (use pictures) of what Northcliffe described as the 'White coal of Ireland'— hundreds of great waterfalls all over the country going to waste, [and] industries of the sort . . . which it could be economic for us to create . . . soap works, great tanneries, beetroot sugar factories,

great frozen meat factories including potted meats. We should
also point out that we have all the raw material in the country for
these things. . . . I have thousands of other possible films in my
mind but these will do to illustrate the line I think these films
should take.[4]

Elsewhere, in published essays, Collins addressed the need
to draw investment capital into Ireland. He focused on the
reinvestment in Ireland of those funds which some Irish people
had placed overseas. His objective was to avoid what he saw as
foreign exploitation of the country's resources.

The Irish people have a large amount of capital invested abroad.
With scope for our energies, with restoration of confidence, the
inevitable tendency will be towards the return of this capital to
Ireland. It will then flow in its proper channel. It will be used for
opening new and promising fields in this country. Ireland will
provide splendid opportunities for the investment of Irish capital,
and it is for the Irish people to take advantage of these
opportunities.

If they do not, investors and exploiters from outside will come
in to reap the rich profits which are to be made. And, what is
worse still, they will bring with them all the evils that we want to
avoid in the new Ireland.

We are a small nation. Our military strength in proportion to
the mighty armaments of modern nations can never be
considerable. Our strength as a nation will depend on our
economic freedom, and upon our moral and intellectual force. In
these we can become a shining light to the world. But Irish men
and women as private individuals must do their share to increase
the prosperity of the country. Business cannot succeed without
capital. Millions of Irish money [sic] are lying idle in banks, the
deposits of Irish joint stock banks increased in the aggregate by
£7,318,000 during the half-year ended 31 December 1921. At that
rate the total of deposits and cash balances in Irish banks was
£194,391,000 to which in addition there was a sum of almost
£14,000,000 in the Post Office Savings Account. If Irish money
were invested in Irish industries, to assist existing ones and to
finance new enterprises, there would be an enormous
development of Irish commerce.[5]

Indeed Collins's love for Ireland is nowhere better displayed than by the expression of his hopes and dreams for the development of the country's full potential and, as we can judge from the following, balanced by a desire not to destroy Ireland's natural beauty and environment, or to lose sight of the fact that the overall welfare of the Irish people must also be taken into account.

What we hope for in the new Ireland is to have such material welfare as will give the Irish spirit that freedom. We want such widely diffused prosperity that the Irish people will not be crushed by destitution into living 'the lives of the beasts'. Neither must they be obliged, owing to an unsound economic condition, to spend all their power of both mind and body in an effort to satisfy the bodily needs alone. The uses of wealth are to provide good health, comfort, moderate luxury, and to give the freedom which comes from the possession of these things.

Our object in building up the country economically must not be lost sight of. That object is not to be able to boast of enormous wealth or of a great volume of trade for their own sakes, nor to see our country covered with smoking chimneys and factories. It is not to show a great national balance sheet, not to point to a people producing wealth with the self-obliteration of a hive of bees.

The real riches of the Irish nation will be the men and women of the Irish nation, the extent to which they are rich in body and mind and character. What we want is the opportunity for everyone to be able to produce sufficient wealth to ensure these advantages for themselves. That such wealth can be produced in Ireland there can be no doubt . . .

If our national economy is put on a sound footing from the beginning, it will in the new Ireland be possible for our people to provide themselves with the ordinary requirements of decent living. It will be possible for each to have sufficient food, a good home in which to live. . . . We shall be able to give our children bodily and mental health, and our people will be able to secure themselves against the inevitable times of sickness and old age.[6]

Given those who have over the course of the past seven

decades sought in one form or another to lay claim to Collins's legacy, the following singularly progressive views he offered in support of an economic justice throughout Irish society call out for special consideration.

That must be our object. What we must aim at is the building of a sound economic life in which great discrepancies cannot occur. We must not have destitution or poverty at one end and at the other an excess of riches in the possession of a few individuals, beyond what they can spend with satisfaction and justification. The growing wealth of Ireland will, we hope, be diffused through all our people, all sharing in the growing prosperity, each receiving what each contributes in the making of that prosperity, so that the wealth of all is ensured.[7]

Collins's vision for Ireland's advancement was also tied to what he saw as a process of incremental change which would in the end produce the country's full independence without resort to further destruction and bloodshed. He was keen to get on with the difficult task of nation building. For Collins, there was also a keen awareness that without economic progress and self-sufficiency, the country's march to full nationhood would be stifled. The following underscores those views, while also offering an insight into his belief that changing international circumstances would lead Britain sooner rather than later to alter its relationship with Ireland.

Looking forward to the operation of world forces to the development of freedom, it is certain that at some time acquiescence in the ultimate separation of the units will come. The American colonies of Britain got their freedom by successful war; Canada, South Africa and the other states of the British Commonwealth are approaching the same by peaceful growth. . . . Separation by peaceful stages of evolution does not expose her and does not endanger her.[8]

It was a view that Collins first expressed in the debate that took place within the Dáil Cabinet, with de Valera present, following the Irish delegation's return after signing the Anglo-Irish Treaty.

The conversion or transformation of Ireland's vast amounts of wasteland into productive use was yet another aspect of the country's development that caught his interest. In Collins's estimate it also offered a significant means for turning the tide against emigration.

> There are some 20 million acres of land in Ireland, and of this about 7 million acres or one-third of the whole consist of waste land and bogs. Walk along the banks of almost any of our rivers and you will find a few fields' depth on each side of that river, and all along its course, are quite useless lands for cultivation. Now, if you can only sink those river-beds and drain those bogs you would bring enough new land into being to stop the national haemorrhage of emigration for the whole of the year. There you have the practical politics of our new day.[9]

Empowering the Irish people to take charge of their own destiny also lay at the centre of his political philosophy. In his view the need for the nation's economic independence was as essential as political freedom.

> We have to build up a new civilisation on the foundations of the old. And here let me say it is not the leaders of the Irish people who can do this for the people. Leaders can only point the way. They can but do their best to establish a reign of justice and of law and order which will enable the people to attain their ideals. The strength of our nation must be the strength of the whole people. We need a political, economic and social system in accordance with our national character. It must be a system in which our material, intellectual and spiritual needs and forces will find the fullest expression and satisfaction.[10]

Of particular relevance to any attempt to grasp the essence of Collins's economic and social vision for the Ireland he wanted to help build is an understanding that what he wanted was an inclusive Ireland, with a society that no doubt was in his mind consistent with the Proclamation of Easter Week's commitment to cherishing 'all the children of the nation'. In the following we see a Collins who was clearly committed to economic justice. It is also the legacy of a man who in all probability would have found little comfort in the reactionary forces in Irish politics that have since sought to usurp his memory.

The Irish nation is the whole people, of every class, creed and outlook. We recognise no distinction. It will be our aim to weld all our people nationally together who have hitherto been divided in political and social and economic outlook. Labour will be free to take its rightful place as an element in the life of the nation. In Ireland, more than in any other country, lies the hope of the rational adjustment of the rights and interests of all sections, and the new government starts with the resolve that Irish labour shall be free to play the part which belongs to it in helping to shape our industrial and commercial future.[11]

Collins offered specific proposals aimed at developing Ireland's resources. His support of a progressive tax system as expressed in the following is also noteworthy.

The keynote to the economic revival must be development of Irish resources by Irish capital for the benefit of the Irish consumer in such a way that the people have steady work at just remuneration and their own share of control.

How are we to develop Irish resources? The earth is our bountiful mother. Upon free access to it depends not only agriculture, but all other trades and industries. Land must be freely available. Agriculture, our main industry, must be improved and developed. Our existing industries must be given opportunities to expand. Conditions must be created which will make it possible for new ones to arise. Means of transit must be extended and cheapened. Our harbours must be developed. Our water power must be utilised; our mineral resources must be exploited.

Foreign trade must be stimulated by making facilities for the transport and marketing of Irish goods abroad and foreign goods in Ireland. Investors must be encouraged to invest Irish capital in Irish concerns. Taxation, where it hinders, must be adjusted and must be imposed where the burdens will fall lightest and can best be borne, and where it will encourage rather than discourage industry . . .

The development of industry in the new Ireland should be on lines that exclude monopoly profits. The product of industry would thus be left sufficiently free to supply good wages to those employed in it. The system should be on cooperative lines rather than on the old commercial capitalistic lines of huge joint stock companies. At the same time, I think we shall avoid state socialism which has nothing to commend it in a country like Ireland, and in any case, is a monopoly of another kind.[12]

Industries targeted by Collins

Given favourable conditions, there is a successful future for dressed meat industries on the lines of the huge cooperative industry started in Wexford; while there are many opportunities for the extension of dairying and cheese-making. The industries we possess are nearly all capable of expansion. We can improve and extend the following:

Brewing and distilling
Manufacture of tobacco
Woollen and linen industry
Manufacture of hosiery and underclothing
Rope and twine industry
Manufacture of boots and shoes, saddlery, and all kinds of other articles
Production of hardware and agricultural machinery
Production and curing of fish.

Of manufactured articles £48,000,000 worth are imported into Ireland yearly. A large part of these could be produced more economically at home. If land were procurable abundantly and cheaply, it would be necessary also that capital should be forthcoming to get suitable sites for factories, a more easily obtained supply of power, an improvement, increase and cheapening of the means of transport.

There are facilities for producing an enormous variety of products for the home and foreign markets, if factories could be established. These should as far as possible be dispersed about the country instead of being concentrated in a few areas. The dispersals will also have the effect of avoiding congestion, but will incidentally improve the status and earnings of the country population and will enlarge their horizons.[13]

Land reform and agriculture policy:

We have now in Ireland, owing to the restrictions put upon emigration during the European War, a larger population of young men and women than we have had for a great many years. For their own sake and to maintain the strength of the nation, room must and can be found for them. Agriculture is, and is likely to continue to be, our chief source of wealth. If room is to be found for our growing population, land must be freely available. Land is not freely available in Ireland. Thousands of acres of the best land lie idle or are occupied as ranches or form part of extensive private estates.

Side by side with this condition, there are thousands of our people who are unable to get land on which to keep a cow or even to provide themselves and their families with vegetables. If the ranches can be broken up, if we can get the land back again into the hands of our people, there will be plenty of employment and a great increase in the national wealth . . .

For those who intend to engage in agriculture, they require specialised education. We have the experience of countries like Holland, Germany and Denmark to guide us. Scientific methods of farming and stock raising must be introduced. We must have the study of specialised chemistry to aid us, as it does our foreign competitors in the countries I have named. We must establish industries arising directly out of agriculture, industries for the utilisation of the by-products of the land: bones, bristles, hides for the production of soda, glue and other valuable substances.

With plenty of land available at an economic rent or price, such industries can be established throughout the country districts, opening up new opportunities for employment . . .

In the development of Ireland, the land question presents itself under four main headings:
1. the completion and purchase of tenanted lands;
2. the extension and increase of powers of purchase of untenanted lands;

3. the question of congestion in rural districts;
4. the utilisation of lands unoccupied or withheld in urban areas.[14]

Developing Ireland's water potential

Water power is concentrated in her 237 rivers and 180 lakes. The huge Lough Corrib system could be utilised, for instance, to work the granite in the neighbourhood of Galway. In the opinion of experts reporting to the Committee on the Water Power Resources of Ireland, from the Irish lakes and rivers a total of 500,000 horse power is capable of being developed.

The magnitude of this is more readily seen if it is appreciated that to raise this power in steam would require 7,500,000 tons of coal. With the present price of coal it should be a commercial proposition to develop our water power as against steam, even though it need not take the place of steam entirely.

Schemes have been worked out to utilise the water power of the Shannon, the Erne, the Bann and the Liffey. It is probable that the Liffey and the Bann, being closely connected with industrial centres, can be dealt with at once. With unified control and direction, various sources of water power could be arranged in large stations for centralised industries, and the energy could be redistributed to provide light and heat for the neighbouring towns and villages . . .

The development of this white power will also enable the means of communication and transport by rail and road to be cheapened and extended. And there is an urgent need for cheap transit. Railway rates and shipping rates are so high that, to take one example, the cost of transit is prohibitive to the Irish fish trade. While the Irish seas are teeming with fish we have the Dublin market depending upon the English fish market for its supplies. The export of Irish fish is decreasing, and the fishing industry is neither the source of remuneration it should be to those engaged in it, nor the source of profit it could be to the country . . .

Our harbours must be developed. Ireland occupies a unique geographical position. She is the stepping stone between the old world and the new. She should therefore become a great exchange mart between Europe and America. With Galway harbour improved and developed so as to receive American liners, passengers could land in Europe two days earlier than by disembarking in Liverpool.[15]

COLLINS ON IRELAND'S CULTURE AND LANGUAGE

Although Michael Collins was not among the ranks of those Irish separatist leaders who were also at the forefront of the effort to revive the Irish language, he none the less possessed a deep love of his native tongue, along with traditional songs and Gaelic games. They formed part of the way of life that was deeply rooted in the rural Irish culture—a culture that was also very much his own. Collins's vision of an independent Ireland clearly included a top place for the restoration of Irish culture and language. It was an objective that was as important to him as the country's material development. In the following he offers an analysis of how British rule brought about the near destruction of Gaelic culture, while outlining his ideas for Ireland's cultural revival. It is a view that is at the centre of his commitment to the 'practical nationalism' he espoused.

The freedom which has been won is the fruit of the national efforts of this generation and of preceding ones. . . . Up to the Union, English interference in Ireland had succeeded only in its military and economic oppression. The national spirit survived . . . The people spoke their own language, preserved their Gaelic customs and way of life, and remained united in their common traditions . . . Entrenched behind their language and their national traditions, they kept their social life intact. . . . With the Union [1800] came upheaval. The seat of government was transferred to England. The garrison which was becoming Gaelicised towards the end of the eighteenth century turned away from Ireland with the destruction of the Dublin Parliament, and made London their capital. . . . The Anglicisation of Ireland had begun. The English language became the language of education. It penetrated slowly at first. It was aided by the national schools. In those schools it was the medium of education for a people who were still Gaelic speaking.

Side by side with this peaceful penetration the Irish language decayed, and when the people had adopted a new language and had come to look to England for government, they learned to see in English customs and English culture the models upon which to fashion their own.

The gifts wrung for Ireland—always wrung by agitation more or less violent in Ireland itself, and never as a result of the oratory of the Irish representatives in the British Parliament—Catholic emancipation, Land Acts, local government, were not actually destructive in themselves of the Gaelic social economic system, but helped in the denationalisation process.

These things undoubtedly brought ameliorative changes, but the people got into the habit of looking to a foreign authority, and they inevitably came to lose their self-respect, their self-reliance and their national strength . . . We lost reverence for our own nation, and we came very close to losing our national identity . . . Until Ireland can speak to the world with a united distinctive voice, we shall not have earned, and shall not get, that full freedom in all its completeness which nations, that are nations, can never rest until they have achieved. . . . only by developing our resources, by linking up our life with the past, and adopting the civilisation which was stopped by the Union could we become Gaels again, and help win our nation back . . . The freedom which Ireland has achieved was dreamed of by Wolfe Tone, was foreseen by Thomas Davis, and their efforts were broadened out until they took into their embrace all the true national movements by the 'grim resolve' of William Rooney, supported later by the 'strong right arms' of the Volunteers.

All the streams—economic, political, spiritual, cultural and militant—met together in the struggle of 1916–1921 which has ended in a peace in which the Treaty of Limerick is wiped out by the departure of the British armed forces, and the establishment of an Irish Army in its place . . . the Union is wiped out by the establishment of a free native parliament which will be erected on a Constitution expressing the will of the Irish people. . . . With the termination of the Union goes national enslavement if we will it. Complete national freedom is ours and nobody but ourselves can prevent us achieving it.

We are free now to get back and keep all that was taken from us. We have no choice but to turn our eyes again to Ireland. The most completely anglicised person in Ireland will look to Britain in vain. Ireland is about to revolve once again on her own axis.[16]

Collins also possessed a practical view as to how the difficult task of reinvigorating native culture in Ireland might be accomplished after years of foreign domination. It is a perspective that also encapsulates a desire to build an Irish culture that is truly egalitarian.

We have now won the first victory . . . We are now free in name. The extent to which we become free in fact and secure our freedom will be the extent to which we become Gaels again. It is a hard task. The machine of the British armed force, which tried to crush us, we could see with our physical eyes. We could touch it. We could put our physical strength against it. We could see their agents in uniform and under arms. We could see their tanks and armoured cars.

But the spiritual machine which has been mutilating us, restoring our customs, and our independent life, is not easy to discern . . . And it has become so familiar, how are we to recognise it? We cannot perhaps. But we can do something else. We can replace it. We can fill our minds with Gaelic ideas, and our lives with Gaelic customs, until there is no room for any other.

It is not any international association with the British nations which is going to hinder us in that task. It lies in our own hands. The survival of some connection with the former enemy, since it has not the power to chain us, should act as a useful irritant . . . We have to build a new civilisation on the foundations of the old. . . . The biggest task will be the restoration of the language. How can we express our most subtle thoughts and finest feelings in a foreign tongue? Irish will scarcely be our language in this generation, not even perhaps in the next. But until we have it again on our tongues and in our minds we are not free, and we will produce no immortal literature.

Our music and art and literature must be in the lives of the people themselves, not as in England, the luxury of a few. England has produced some historians, many great poets and a few great artists, but they are the treasures of the cultured minority and have no place in the lives of the main body of the English people.

Our poets and artists will be inspired in the stimulating air of freedom to be something more than the mere producers of verse and painters of pictures. They will teach us, by their vision, the noble race we may become. They will inspire us to live as Irish men and Irish women should. . . . Our civilisation will be glorious or the reverse, according to the character of the people. And the work we produce will be the expression of what we are. Our external life has become the expression of all that we are deprived of—something shapeless, ugly, without native life. . . . Irish art and Irish customs must be carried out by the people themselves, helped by a central government, not controlled and managed by it, helped by departments of music, art, national painting, etc., with local centres connected with them.[17]

THE DEATH OF
COLLINS

'There seems to be a malignant fate dogging the fortunes of Ireland, for at every critical period in her story, the man whom the country trusts is taken from her.'[1]

C ollins's comments, made after the sudden death of his friend Arthur Griffith, could just as well have been uttered by another about him on the day after his assassination in west Cork.

A unique insight into Collins's actions and indeed machinations at the end of his life is provided by two men on opposite sides of the Irish struggle: Erskine Childers and Lionel Curtis. The former had become an Irish patriot; the other remained a staunch British imperialist. The two had themselves crossed paths when Childers served as Clerk to the House of Commons and Curtis as a chief strategist for the Liberal Party. Later Curtis would serve as an architect of the British Commonwealth system. But they became enemies as Curtis remained a defender of the Empire and a key legal adviser to Lloyd George and the Coalition, while Childers openly defected to the cause of Irish independence. He won the confidence of Éamon de Valera, becoming secretary to the Irish delegation to the October 1921 Anglo-Irish Conference. An added note of irony was the fact that as Childers sided with de Valera against Collins and the latter fought to defend the Treaty with the British Government, Collins drew closer to Curtis's orbit as he became an open opponent of Childers. The assessments offered by Childers and Curtis in the aftermath of Collins's death serve from opposite perspectives to help clarify Collins's actions at the end of his life. First, we hear from Childers's eulogy of Collins, rendered in the republican organ, *An Poblacht*. Childers would himself meet death at the hands of an Irishman not long afterwards. For him it would be before a Free State firing squad as a political prisoner. Childers had been arrested by the Free State Army for the possession of a small revolver that Collins had in fact given him for his own protection during the War of Independence.

> Like a gallant soldier he [Collins] took the risk of that perilous passage through hostile country—and like a gallant soldier he fell on the field of action . . . His buoyant energy, his organising powers, immense industry, acute and subtle intelligence . . . charm and gift of oratory . . . he flung without stint into the republican cause for five years . . .
>
> What was his dominant motive? There may have been a bias due to ambition—the glamour of a career like that of Jan Smuts[*] —but standing now at his grave few will be ungenerous enough to doubt that his ruling motive and sincere belief was that the Treaty was a necessary halting place on the road to a recognised Republic, that it gave us freedom to achieve freedom which was beyond the power of Ireland now to wrest from her mighty enemy.[2]

([*]Jan Smuts, former leader of the Boers in their war of independence against Britain, became Prime Minister of a South African state within the British Commonwealth, and indeed worked at Britain's request to help persuade Sinn Féin in June 1921 to accept approximate dominion status for Ireland within the British Empire.)

In the case of Lionel Curtis, despite having the responsibility thrust on him by history and circumstance to assist Britain in its effort to carry out its obligations under the Anglo-Irish Treaty, it is clear from his personal remarks to British officials in the aftermath of Collins's death that he held little faith in Collins's overall motives towards Britain. His first utterance was made to Andy Cope on 23 August 1922—the day after Collins's assassination. Its sarcasm towards the end is palpable.

I got your message in bed at 6.20 this morning . . . On reaching the office I at once commenced a meeting of Sturgis, Tallants, Stephenson and Hill and laid your messages before them. During this meeting Miss Collins [Collins's sister] came in to know if the news were true and after asking me to telegraph you for particulars about the next of kin, etc., gave me the information she wanted. . . . Collins once said here that the best service he could render the RIC would be to get murdered, which was fine of him. He was such a lovable creature and my heart bleeds for his young woman.[3]

Yet it was Curtis's remarks made as an aside to Winston Churchill in a correspondence concerning the Boundary Commission almost two years to the date of Collins's death that are particularly useful in shedding light on what may well have been a prevalent British official view of Collins.

I have never thought that Collins tried to meet you squarely on the Treaty. I am not sure he was responsible for those atrocities— but his own hands were so red with blood he could not bring himself to the murder of British soldiers very sincerely except when it threatened his own political power.[4]

CONCLUSION

His was a loss that still cannot be fully weighed. But we can try to understand this talented, complex, driven, and often tortured young man better. In the preceding, by presenting many of his public and private thoughts, we have tried to make that task easier.

What we have left are his words. We have no physical record of his rich, chuckling voice, heavily laced with the accent of west Cork. We cannot see him suddenly jolting his head back to clear a shock of thick black hair from his eyes, or watch him tapping the table with his pen as he sat deep in thought, or witness a sudden outburst of temper. But as we look at the vision he offered for Ireland seven decades ago, we see a man presenting ideas that were his own. There are no bromides, no shibboleths. There are no speech-writers or handlers. There are only his own ideas, some more formed than others, but offering clear evidence of a man who was evolving and learning with the passage of time and of a man who was governed by the democratic wishes of the Irish people.

The ideas contained herein form the essence of Michael Collins's commitment to Ireland and to all its children. It is a commitment that continues to challenge those from every walk of life and corner of this island who believe, as he did, that Ireland's best days are yet to come.

9

VINTAGE COLLINS

Michael Collins possessed a keen intelligence and quick wit to go with his abundance of energy. But he also provoked strong feelings among his colleagues that often led to grudges being carried against him long after he had forgotten an outburst he had delivered against a hapless recipient. Such was often the case as Frank O'Connor noted in his biography of Collins. None the less, while the moniker 'The Big Fellow' was bestowed upon him in a pejorative light to characterise what some saw as his degree of bluster, over time it became a term of admiration for others. Thus when Austin Stack remarked after one particular bout of criticism by Collins that 'He's no big fellow to me', he did so forgetting the origins of the title. In the following, these samples of Collins's caustic wit, brutal honesty and basic humanity are offered to help round out this portrait of the man in his own words.

'If there is a God, I defy him.'
(Cited in Frank O'Connor, *The Big Fellow*, p. 4.)

'Without guns you might as well be dead.'
(Cited in León Ó Broin, *Michael Collins*, p. 84.)

'They said we were drunk in '98. They won't be able to say that now.'
(Collins inside the GPO after emptying the contents of the beer kegs he found in storage in the building during Easter Week.)

'I'm the only man in the whole place who wasn't at Confession or Communion!'
(Collins inside the GPO during the Easter Rising, 1916, Frank O'Connor, *The Big Fellow*, p. 15.)

'You're doing great work lads!'
(Collins to Vinnie Byrne and other members of the 'squad', his handpicked band of assassins, Tim Pat Coogan, *Michael Collins*, p. 116.)

'I never realised there was so much cowardice, dishonesty, hedging insincerity and meanness in the world.'
(Collins, as quoted in Béaslaí, *Michael Collins and the Making of a New Ireland*, Vol. 1, pp 358–9.)

'I found that those fellows we put on the spot were going to put a lot of us on the spot, so I got there first.'
(In explaining the assassination of British secret agents, Bloody Sunday, 21 November 1920.)

'Good God. We're finished now. It's all up.'
(Upon learning that IRA men Dick McKee and Peader Clancy had been killed in Dublin Castle by British forces the night before Bloody Sunday.)

'When will it all end? When can a man get down to a book and peace?'
(Collins to Joe O'Reilly on Bloody Sunday, 20 November 1920, Taylor, p. 13.)

'Our propaganda can never be stronger than our actions at home.'
(Frank O'Connor, *The Big Fellow*, p. 51.)

'Long hoor.'
(A description by Collins of Éamon de Valera.).

'You'll get none of my men for that.'
(In response to a plan by Cathal Brugha to bomb and machine-gun civilian crowds in British theatres and cinemas.)

'The poor kid!'
(Collins upon hearing that his attempt to effect an escape for
Kevin Barry on 1 November 1920 had failed and that the
18-year old had been hanged in Mountjoy Jail.)

'There is no crime in detecting and destroying in wartime
the spy and the informer. They have destroyed without trial.
I have paid them back in their own coin.'
(Michael Collins, quoted in Rex Taylor, *Michael Collins*.)

'To go for a drink is one thing. To be driven to it is another.'
(Michael Collins to John O'Kane, November 1921, as cited
by Coogan, p. 242.)

'My bail is up. They're looking for me.'
(Collins to Ernie O'Malley in Dublin, Spring 1919.)

'This is a real nest of singing birds. They chirrup mightily
one to the other—and there's the falseness of it all, because
no one trusts the other.'
(Collins to John O'Kane, 23 October 1921, during an early
phase of the Anglo-Irish Conference.)

'You cannot create a republic overnight.'
(Collins to John O'Kane, 17 October 1921.)

'I don't know what the hell it is!'
(Collins in response to the rest of the Irish delegation's
bewilderment over a secret letter from Arthur Griffith to
Lloyd George pledging not to 'break' over Ulster, 8
December 1921.)

'You'll be seeing from the papers that the Sinn Féin clubs are
going strongly republican—and the places. Such places!
Tralee after the Auxies had gone, Galway the same. God
help us from them. They're beauties.'
(Collins to Kitty Kiernan, 29 January 1922, as cited in León
Ó Broin, *In Great Haste*, p. 105.)

'I wish we had the bishops against us.'
(Collins remarking on his discomfort in 1922 that so many of the Catholic bishops who opposed his colleagues and him during the War of Independence were now on the side of the Free State.)

'Anybody who is out for blood or scalps is of little use to the country; equally, of course, the real issue cannot be departed from.'
(Collins in a letter to a friend before his death, as cited in *An T-Oglach*, 26 August 1922.)

'There seems to be a malignant fate dogging the fortunes of Ireland, for at every critical period in her story the man whom the country trusts is taken from her.'
(Collins following the death of Arthur Griffith, the *Irish Independent*, 14 August 1922.)

NOTES

CHAPTER 1 THE YOUNG MICHAEL COLLINS (pp 1–6)
1. Frank O'Connor, *Field Day Anthology of Irish Writing*, Vol. III, New York, 1992, p. 478.
2. Hayden Talbot, *Michael Collins' Own Story*, New York, 1923, p. 23.
3. Ibid, pp 12–13.
4. Essay by Collins, 1906, written while he attended Clonakilty National School, Collins Papers, NLI.
5. Talbot, *Michael Collins' Own Story*, p. 25.
6. Rex Taylor, *Michael Collins*, London, 1958, p. 32.
7. Margery Forester, *Michael Collins: The Lost Leader*, London, 1971, p. 30.

CHAPTER 2 COLLINS AT WAR: THE TRUCE (pp 7–31)
1. Collins to Hannie Collins in Margery Forester, *Michael Collins: The Lost Leader*, London, 1971, p. 34.
2. Craig Gardner, Chartered Accountants, to Frank O'Connor, 21 July 1936, Dáil Éireann Files, PRO, Dublin, DE2/292.
3. Collins to Kevin O'Brien, 10 June 1916 in Rex Taylor, *Michael Collins*, London, 1958, p. 58.
4. Sean O'Mahoney, *Frongoch: University of Revolution*, Dublin, 1987, p. 62.
5. Ibid, p. 40.

6. Austin Stack was Deputy Chief of Staff of the IRA and Minister for Home Affairs in the Dáil Cabinet. He set up the Republican Courts in 1920. During the Easter Rising, 1916, he was Commandant of the Volunteers in Kerry which failed to connect with the *Aud* for the receipt of arms and ammunition from Germany. He was imprisoned at length periodically between April 1916 and autumn 1919, and escaped from Manchester afterwards. He was elected as a member for North Munster, member of the IRB executive, and in November 1918 as MP for Kerry in the general election; from there he served in Dáil Éireann. He broke with Collins over the Anglo-Irish Treaty, but it was apparent that a serious rift had developed prior to the 1921 Anglo-Irish Conference.

7. Collins to Austin Stack, 6 June 1918, Collins Papers, NLI, MS. 5848.

8. Collins to Michael Lacey, mid-Limerick Brigade Commandant, 15 May 1918 in Rex Taylor, *Michael Collins*, London, 1958, p. 80.

9. Collins to Austin Stack, 27 July 1918, Collins Papers, NLI, MS. 5848.

10. Ibid, 11 February 1919.

11. Ibid, 18 May 1919.

12. Ibid (No. 23), 12 September 1919.

13. Ibid.

14. Ibid, 21 August 1918.

15. Ibid, 18 November 1918.

16. Ibid, 10 October 1918.

17. Ibid, 11 November 1918.

18. Ibid, 18 May 1919.

19. Collins to Frank Barrett, 8 August 1919 (Military History Bureau, Department of Defence, A/O362).

20. Taylor, *Michael Collins*, p. 78.

21. Collins to Michael Lacey, mid-Limerick Brigade Commandant, 6 October 1919, Collins Papers, NLI.

22. Taylor, *Michael Collins*, p. 81.

23. Collins Papers, NLI.

24. Taylor, *Michael Collins*, p. 77.

25. Frank O'Connor, *The Big Fellow*, Dublin, 1968 ed., p. 98.

26. Francis Costello, *Enduring the Most: The Life and Death of Terence MacSwiney*, Dublin, 1995, p. 161.

27. Collins to Art O'Brien, 25 September 1920, Dáil Éireann Files, PRO, Dublin.
28. Ibid, 25 and 28 September 1920.
29. Hayden Talbot, *Michael Collins' Own Story*, New York, 1923, p. 93.
30. Collins to Richard Mulcahy, 7 April 1922, Richard Mulcahy Collection, University College, Dublin.
31. Ibid.
32. Ibid, 26 March 1921.
33. Collins to William O'Brien, 6 July 1921, William O'Brien Collection, NLI.
34. Collins to Liam Tobin, 1921, Piaras Béaslaí, *Michael Collins and the Making of a New Ireland*, Vol. 1, p. 336.
35. Collins to Acting Commandant, Cork No. 1 Brigade, 8 January 1920, Military History Bureau, Department of Defence, A/O498/11.
36. Frank Crozier, *Ireland Forever*, London, 1932, pp 219–20.
37. Taylor, *Michael Collins*, p. 82.
38. Collins to Richard Mulcahy, 15 April 1921, Mulcahy Collection, UCD.
39. Ibid.
40. Collins to Liam Lynch, 2 January 1920, Military History Bureau, Dept of Defence, A/O499/IV.
41. Ibid, 5 April 1920, A/O499/SVIII.
42. Collins to Acting Brigade Commandant, Cork No. 1 Brigade, 8 January 1920, Military History Bureau, Dept of Defence, A/O498/II.
43. Collins to Sean Fitzpatrick, Commandant, No. 10 Wing, Cork Jail, 15 April 1920, Military History Bureau, Dept of Defence, A/O498/XI.
44. O'Connor, *The Big Fellow*, p. 55.
45. Frank O'Connor, *My Father's Son*, New York, 1969, p. 140.
46. Michael Collins, *The Path to Freedom*, Dublin, 1922, pp 73–4.
47. Collins to de Valera, 19 July 1921 in Tim Pat Coogan, *Michael Collins: A Life*, London, 1990 ed., p. 222.
48. Ibid.
49. Collins to Art O'Brien, 17 August 1921, Coogan, *Michael Collins*.

CHAPTER 3 COLLINS THE MAN (pp 32–39)

1. Collins to de Valera, 19 April and 6 May 1921, Dáil Éireann Files, PRO, Dublin.
2. Rex Taylor, *Michael Collins*, London, 1958, p. 135–6.
3. Ibid, p. 136.
4. León Ó Broin, *In Great Haste*, Dublin, 1996, pp 39–40.
5. Michael Collins to Carl Ackerman, 6 April 1921, as submitted by Sir Hamar Greenwood to Lloyd George on 21 April 1921, Lloyd George Collection, HLRO, F/19/3/19.
6. Ibid.
7. Collins's notes, as cited in Taylor, *Michael Collins*, p. 123.
8. Ibid, p. 124.
9. Ibid, p. 123.
10. Ibid.
11. Ibid, p. 124.
12. Michael Collins, *The Path to Freedom*, p. 120.
13. Ibid, pp 124–5.

CHAPTER 4 COLLINS AND FINANCE (pp 40–54)

1. Garret FitzGerald, from an interview with the author, 12 April 1989.
2. Dáil Éireann Minutes, 19 May 1919, pp 94–5.
3. Ronan Fanning, *The Irish Department of Finance 1922–1958*, Dublin, 1978, p. 21.
4. Ibid, p. 21.
5. Dáil Éireann Files, 2/7, PRO, Dublin; and Fanning, *Department of Finance*, p. 22.
6. Collins to Éamon de Valera, 18 February 1921, Dáil Éireann Files, PRO, Dublin.
7. Ibid, 4 February 1921.
8. Dáil Éireann Loan Prospectus, issued by the Dept of Finance, Dáil Éireann Files, PRO, Dublin.
9. Collins to de Valera, cited in Piaras Béaslaí, *Michael Collins and the Making of a New Ireland*, Vol. I, pp 357 and 413–14.
10. Ibid, pp 414–16.
11. Collins to Terence MacSwiney, 25 September 1919, Dáil Éireann Files, PRO, Dublin.
12. Ibid, 29 March 1920.
13. Ibid, 9 April 1920.
14. Ibid, 21 April 1920.
15. Francis Costello, *Enduring the Most: The Life and Death of Terence MacSwiney*, Dublin, 1995.

16. Frank O'Connor, *The Big Fellow*, Dublin, 1968 ed., p. 56.
17. Statement of Collins as Minister for Finance, 7 July 1920, Mulcahy Collection, UCD, P48b/405.
18. Fanning, *Department of Finance*, p. 21.
19. Collins to Art O'Brien, 10 February 1920 (Collins Papers), NLI, MS. 8430.
20. Éamon de Valera to Collins, 7 January 1921, Dáil Éireann Files, PRO, Dublin.
21. Collins to de Valera, 7 January 1921, Dáil Éireann Files, PRO, Dublin.
22. Fanning, *Department of Finance*, p. 18.
23. Ibid.
24. Private Session, 17 September 1920, Dáil Éireann Files, PRO, Dublin.
25. Report of Collins as Minister for Finance to Dáil Éireann, 31 December 1920, Mulcahy Collection, UCD.
26. Ibid.
27. Collins to P. O'Keefe, 21 January 1921, Dáil Éireann Files, PRO, Dublin.
28. Collins to de Valera, 1 June 1921, Dáil Éireann Files, PRO, Dublin.
29. Ibid, 7 January 1921.
30. Ibid.
31. Dáil Éireann Papers, 2/304, Part III, PRO, Dublin.
32. Fanning, *Department of Finance*, p. 33.
33. Ibid, p. 55.
34. Ibid, p. 57.

CHAPTER 5 COLLINS: DEMOCRATIC POLITICS, PARTITION AND THE NORTH (pp 55–65)

1. Michael Collins, *The Path to Freedom*, Cork, 1968 ed., pp 61–2.
2. From 'Election Day Directions for Sinn Féin Workers', prepared by Collins in 1921, Collins Papers, NLI.
3. Ibid.
4. Frank O'Connor, *The Big Fellow*, Dublin, 1968 ed., p. 174.
5. Hayden Talbot, *Michael Collins' Own Story*, New York, 1923, pp 74–5.
6. Collins to Arthur Griffith, August 1921, Dáil Éireann Files, PRO, Dublin.
7. Collins, *Path to Freedom*, p. 3.
8. Ibid.

9. Ibid.
10. Collins to Winston Churchill, in Gilbert (ed.), *Winston Churchill: The Stricken World*, p. 741.
11. Ibid (9 August 1922), p. 744.

CHAPTER 6 COLLINS: THE TREATY, FREE STATE AND CIVIL WAR (pp 66–96)
1. Francis Costello, *Enduring the Most: The Life of Terence MacSwiney*, Dublin, 1994, p. 116.
2. The best account is found in de Valera's own words in Sean Cronin's *The McGarrity Papers*, Tralee, 1972, in remarks addressed to Clan na Gael leader Joe McGarrity in Philadelphia.
3. Dáil Éireann Minutes, Private Session, 14 September 1921.
4. Manuscript of Sean Ó Muirithile, Mulcahy Collection, UCD.
5. Ibid.
6. Lionel Curtis to Lloyd George, 21 September 1921, Tom Jones Collection, National Library of Wales, File CG.
7. Irish Delegation to President de Valera, 26 October 1921, Erkine Childers Collection, TCD, 7790.
8. For a wider discussion of these and related matters, see Francis Costello, 'The Irish Representatives to the London Anglo-Irish Conference in 1921: Violators of the Authority or Victims of Contradictory Instructions?', *Eire-Ireland*, Summer 1989, Vol. XXIX, No. 2, pp 52–78.
9. Tim Pat Coogan, *Michael Collins: A Life*, London, 1990.
10. Frank Pakenham, *Peace By Ordeal*, London, 1972 ed., p. 226.
11. Rex Taylor, *Michael Collins*, London, 1958, p. 131.
12. 'Rough Minutes from Anglo-Irish Conference', 14 October 1921, Erskine Childers Collection, TCD, 7799/7802.
13. Pakenham, *Peace*, p. 134.
14. Collins to Kitty Kiernan, 15 November 1921, Letter 45, cited by León Ó Broin, *In Great Haste*, Dublin, 1996 ed., p. 64.
15. Coogan, *Michael Collins*, p. 242.
16. Taylor, *Michael Collins*, pp 142–3.
17. Ibid.
18. Ibid.

19. Ibid.
20. Minutes of a meeting of the Cabinet and Delegation, 3 December 1921, as compiled by Colm O'Murchada, Assistant Secretary of the Dáil Cabinet, PRO, Dublin, P4/492.
21. Pakenham, *Peace*, p. 224.
22. León Ó Broin, *Michael Collins*, Dublin, 1982, p. 113.
23. Dáil Debates, December 1922.
24. Dáil Debates.
25. Ibid, December 1921.
26. Treaty Debates, Private Session, 17 December 1921, pp 260–61.
27. Collins, Dáil Debates, Private Session, 14 December 1921, p. 138.
28. Dáil Éireann, Private Session, 17 December 1921, pp 260–61.
29. Ibid, 14 December 1921, p. 135.
30. Ibid, December 1921.
31. Collins to Kitty Kiernan, 6 December 1921, in Ó Broin, *In Great Haste*, p. 85.
32. Ibid, pp 95–6.
33. Dáil Debates, Public Session, 19 December 1921, p. 35.
34. Ibid, p. 36.
35. Public statement of Collins in Dublin, 5 March 1922, as published in Collins, *Arguments for the Treaty*, Dublin, 1922, pp 9–18.
36. Ibid.
37. Ibid.
38. Public statement of Collins in Cork city, 12 March 1922, as published in Collins, *Arguments*, pp 18–19.
39. See Michael Hopkinson, *Green Against Green: The Irish Civil War*, Dublin, 1988, pp 115–22.
40. Statement of Collins on the bombardment of the Four Courts, 28 June 1922, Dáil Éireann Files, PRO, Dublin, S 1322.
41. Collins in Frank O'Connor, *The Big Fellow*, Dublin, 1968 ed., pp 170–71.
42. From the record of US Senator James D. Phelan from a meeting with Collins, 31 July 1922, Phelan Collection, University of California at Berkeley.
43. Ó Broin, *Michael Collins*, pp 83–4.
44. Taylor, *Michael Collins*, p. 194.

45. Ó Broin, *In Great Haste*, p. 219.
46. Eoin Neeson, *The Life and Death of Michael Collins*, Cork, 1968, p. 120.
47. Margery Forester, *Michael Collins: The Lost Leader*, London, 1971, p. 334.

CHAPTER 7 COLLINS'S VISION FOR IRELAND (pp 97–110)
1. Collins to Desmond FitzGerald, 12 July 1922, Dáil Éireann Files, PRO, Dublin.
2. Ibid.
3. Ibid.
4. Ibid.
5. Collins, *The Path to Freedom*, Dublin, 1922, pp 116–17.
6. Ibid, pp 127–41.
7. Ibid.
8. Ibid, p. 88.
9. Collins, *'Clearing the Road': An Essay in Practical Politics*, Dublin, 1922.
10. Ibid.
11. Collins, *The Path to Freedom*, Dublin, 1968 ed., pp 25–6.
12. Ibid.
13. Ibid, pp 109–12.
14. Ibid, pp 110–12.
15. Ibid, pp 113–15.
16. Ibid, pp 118–26.
17. Ibid, pp 100–105.

CHAPTER 8 THE DEATH OF COLLINS (pp 111–114)
1. Collins after the death of Arthur Griffith, *Irish Independent*, 14 August 1922.
2. Erskine Childers in *An Poblacht*, September 1922.
3. Lionel Curtis to Any Cope, 23 August 1922, Tom Jones Collection, National Library of Wales, Class CG.
4. Lionel Curtis to Winston Churchill, 19 August 1924, Tom Jones Collection, National Library of Wales, Class CG.

BIBLIOGRAPHY

Private Papers, Documents and Publications

Ernest Blythe Collection, University College, Dublin.
Erskine Childers Collection, Trinity College, Dublin.
Colonial Office Papers, British Public Records Office, Kew
Michael Collins Papers, National Library of Ireland.
Dáil Éireann Files, Public Records Office, Dublin.
Tom Jones Collection, National Library of Wales.
Bonar Law Collection, House of Lords Records Office.
Dáil Éireann Minutes, 1919–1922, Public and Private Sessions.
Lloyd George Collection, House of Lords Records Office, Westminster.
Richard Mulcahy Collection, University College, Dublin.
William O'Brien Collection, National Library of Ireland.
Hugh O'Kennedy Papers, University College, Dublin.
James Phelan Collection, University of California at Berkeley

Books

Béaslaí, Piaras, *Michael Collins and the Making of a New Ireland*, 2 vols (Dublin, 1927).
Churchill, Winston, *The Stricken World*.
Collins, Michael, *The Path to Freedom* (Dublin, 1922).
Collins, Michael, *The Path to Freedom* (Mercier, 1968 ed.).

BIBLIOGRAPHY

Collins, Michael, *Arguments for the Treaty* (Dublin, 1922).
Coogan, Tim Pat, *Michael Collins: A Life* (London, 1990 ed.).
Costello, Francis, *Enduring the Most: The Life and Death of Terence MacSwiney* (Dublin, 1995).
Crozier, Frank, *Ireland Forever* (London, 1932).
Dwyer, T. R., *Michael Collins* (Cork, 1990).
Fanning, Ronan, *The Irish Department of Finance 1922–1958* (Dublin, 1978).
Forester, Margery, *Michael Collins: The Lost Leader* (London, 1971).
Neeson, Eoin, *The Life and Death of Michael Collins* (Cork, 1968).
Ó Broin, León, *Michael Collins* (Dublin, 1982).
Ó Broin, León, *In Great Haste: The Letters of Michael Collins and Kitty Kiernan*; revised and extended by Cian Ó hÉigeartaigh, (Dublin, 1996).
O'Connor, Frank, *The Big Fellow* (Dublin, 1968 ed.).
O'Connor, Frank, *My Father's Son* (New York, 1969).
O'Mahoney, Sean, *Frongoch: University of Revolution* (Dublin, 1987).
Pakenham, Frank, *Peace By Ordeal* (London, 1972 ed.).
Talbot, Hayden, *Michael Collins' Own Story* (New York, 1923).
Taylor, Rex, *Michael Collins* (London, 1958).

NEWSPAPERS

The Irish Times, 1916–1922
Irish Independent, 1918–1922
An Poblacht, 1922
Cork Examiner, 1918–1922
Freeman's Journal, 1918–1921

INDEX

Ackerman, Carl, 35
agriculture, 105–6
Anglo-Irish Treaty, 1921, 22, 32,
    41, 52
  talks, 33, 35–7, 53, 66–79
  partition, 61–3
  Collins proposal, 72–4
  signed, 78–9
  Dáil debates, 79–85, 101
  election campaign, 86–8
Antrim, County, 74
Armagh, County, 23, 57, 60

Barrett, Frank, 17
Barry, Kevin, 19, 22
Barton, Robert, 83–4
Belfast Jail, 11
Bell, RM Alan, 43
Birkenhead, Lord, 74
Black and Tans, 49
Blewith, Mr, 3
Bloody Sunday, 1920, 20–22,
    28–9
Blythe, Ernest, 92
boglands, 102
Boland, Harry, 16–17, 68, 94–5
Bonar Law, Andrew, 30
Boundary Commission, 62,
    63–5, 78, 84, 113
Breen, Dan, 16
Brennan, Frank, 14
British army, 23, 89–90. see also
    War of Independence
Brugha, Cathal, 33–4, 52, 72, 77
Bulgaria, 15

Chamberlain, Austen, 36, 70
Childers, Erskine, 33, 47, 69–70,
    74, 80, 111–12
Churchill, Winston, 63, 64, 89,
    90, 92
  Collins on, 36
  Treaty talks, 74, 83, 113
civil service, 4, 54
Civil War, 29, 54, 63, 66, 89–96
Clan na Gael, 44
Clare, County, 14, 17, 56–7
Clarke, Kathleen, 45
Clarke, Tom, 6, 8, 9, 39
Clonakilty National School, 2–4,
    72
Clune, Archbishop Patrick, 22
Cohalan, Dr, Bishop of Cork, 47
Collins, Con, 10
Collins, Hanna, 3, 7
Collins, Michael. see also Anglo-
    Irish Treaty; Civil War; War
    of Independence
  childhood, 1–4
  employment, 4–5
  joins IRB, 5, 6
  Easter Rising, 7–9
  Prisoners' Association, 9–10
  booklist, 10
  and Sinn Féin, 10, 12–14
  army command, 13–14,
    17–19, 23–4, 26–8
  Finance Minister, 13–14, 19,
    33, 40–54, 60
  international interests, 15
  attitude to violence, 16–17,
    20–21, 25–6, 28–9

Collins, Michael, *contd*
  Intelligence Director, 20–22,
    24–6, 43
  Truce, 29–31
  relations with de Valera,
    30–31, 32–3, 51–2, 66,
    93–4
  relations with Griffith, 33–4,
    38–9, 41, 48, 61–2
  use of press, 34–5
  judgment of others, 35–9
  escapes, 51–2
  Provisional Government,
    53–4
  election campaigns, 55–60
  and partition, 60–65
  Treaty talks, 66–79
  Treaty debates, 79–85
  vision for Ireland, 97–110
  tributes to, 111–14
  quotes from, 115–18
Collins, Michael Snr, 2
Collins, Miss, 113
Connolly, James, 8
conscription, 6
Cope, Andy, 112–13
Cork, County, 14, 22, 25,
    30–31, 69
  IRA brigades, 27–8
  Dáil Loan, 46
  Collins visit, 95–6
Cork city, 30, 67, 93
Cork Jail, 20, 28
Craig, Sir James, 63, 64–5, 78,
    86, 92
Croke Park shootings, 22
Crowe, Maurice, 27
Crowley, Mr, 3
Cullen, Liam, 64
cultural policy, 107–10
Cumann na mBan, 59
Curtis, Lionel, 70, 111, 112–13

Dáil Éireann, 13–14, 22–3, 60
  inaugural session, 16
  Collins on, 16–17

Dáil Loan, 41–50
  finances, 49–53
  Treaty debates, 66, 79–85,
    101
Davis, Thomas, 37, 38, 108
De Roiste, Liam, 47
de Valera, Éamon, 10, 16, 61,
    96, 111
  return from USA, 22, 32, 49,
    52
  relations with Collins, 30–33,
    51–2, 66, 93–4
  USA fund-raising, 41, 44,
    45–6, 48
  Dáil finances, 42–3, 44–6,
    49–50
  Document No. 2, 55, 56–7,
    59, 69–70, 80–83
  Lloyd George talks, 68, 69
  and Treaty talks, 70–72, 75,
    77
  Treaty debates, 79–83, 101
  Treaty election, 86–8
de Valera, Sinead, 32, 52
Defence, Ministry of, 52
Democratic Programme, 44
Derry, County, 23, 65
Document No. 2, 69–70, 80–81,
    82–3
Dominion Status, 31, 74, 112
Donegal, County, 74
Down, County, 23, 46, 74
Dublin Brigade, IRA, 21
Dublin Castle, 24, 35, 54
Duggan, Eamonn, 36

Easter Rising, 1916, 7–9, 55, 56,
    102
economic development, 98–101
External Association, 70–71, 72,
    74

Fanning, Ronan, 40, 49
Fermanagh, County, 46, 65, 74,
    78
film, 44–5, 97–8

Finance, Department of
First Dáil, 13–14, 19, 33,
40–43, 61
Irish Free State, 40
Dáil Loan, 41–50
fisheries, 98, 106
FitzGerald, Desmond, 97, 98
FitzGerald, Garret, 40
Fogarty, Dr, Bishop of Killaloe,
47
Four Courts occupation, 64,
89–91
Free State Army, 54, 90, 95
Frongoch camp, 9

Gaelic Athletic Association
(GAA), 5, 59
Gaelic League, 59
Galway, County, 23, 26, 46
Gavan Duffy, George, 36
general elections
1918, 13, 55, 59–60
1921, 57–9
Government of Ireland Act
1920, 60
Great Famine, 73
Greenwood, Sir Hamar, 35, 36
Griffith, Arthur, 10, 20, 22, 65,
87
Treaty talks, 31, 36, 67, 68,
70–71, 74–7
relations with Collins, 33–4,
38–9, 41, 48, 61–2
Dáil Loan, 44
Treaty debates, 80
Dáil President, 86
death of, 92, 95, 111
Guarantee Trust Company, 4

Hannigan, D., 10
Healy, 11
Horne, Sir Robert, 53
hunger-strikes, 19–20, 22, 25
Hunt, 14

industrial development, 98–9,
104–5
Irish Congress of Trade Unions,
24
Irish Free State, 21–2, 59, 62, 66
finances, 41, 53–4
Collins's role, 85–8
Irish language, 1, 5, 38, 109
Irish Parliamentary Party, 56, 59
Irish Republican Army (IRA),
16, 60, 61, 67
prisoners, 19–20, 25
Bloody Sunday, 1920, 20–21,
28–9
organisation, 23–4, 26–8
funding, 42, 44, 49
Wilson assassination, 64
Civil War, 89–96
Irish Republican Brotherhood
(IRB), 5, 6, 13, 69
Irish Republican Party, 59
Irish Volunteers, 5, 10–11, 13. see
also Irish Republican Army
Easter Rising, 8–9
War of Independence, 16,
18–19

Kerry, County, 12, 14
Kiernan, Kitty, 34, 67, 68, 75–6,
84, 95
Kilmichael, Co. Cork, 22

land reform, 105–6
League of Nations, 72
Limerick, County, 10–11, 14,
27, 46
Lindsay, Mrs, 25–6
Lloyd George, David, 9, 22, 30,
35, 111
offer of talks, 31, 61–2, 79
Collins on, 36
Treaty talks, 63, 70–71, 74–7,
82–3
de Valera talks, 68, 69
Longford, County, 56

Lynch, Fionan, 12
Lynch, Liam, 27, 93

McCormack, Patrick, 21, 22
MacCurtain, Tomás, 67
Mac Diarmada, Seán, 6, 8–9, 39
McGuinness, Joe, 55, 56
Macready, General, 35, 90
MacSwiney, Terence, 27–8, 67
    hunger-strike, 19–20, 22, 25
    Dáil Loan, 46–7
Mayo, County, 26
Meath, County, 17
media, 34–5
    film, 44–5, 97–8
Mountjoy Jail, 19, 25
Mulcahy, Richard, 14, 21, 23–4,
    26

Northern Ireland (NI), 46, 59,
    86–7, 92
    and Collins, 60–65
    in Treaty talks, 74–5, 76, 78
    in Treaty, 84–5

O'Brien, Art, 19–20, 31, 49
O'Brien, William, 24
O'Connell, Daniel, 37–8
O'Connell, General J.J., 90–91
O'Connor, Batt, 42, 49
O'Connor, Frank, 1, 29, 48, 59
O'Connor, James, 13
O'Connor, Rory, 64, 89
Official Secrets Act, 54
O'Flanagan, Fr Michael, 22
Oglach, An t-, 19
O'Grady, Sean, 17
O'Higgins, Kevin, 63
O'Kane, John, 33, 78
O'Kelly, Sean T., 42–3
O'Reilly, Joe, 29

Paris Peace Conference, 16, 40
Pearse, Margaret, 45
Pearse, Patrick, 8, 45

Pearse, Willie, 45
Phelan, Senator James D., 92–4
Phoblacht, An, 112
Plunkett, Count, 7, 55, 56
Plunkett, Joseph, 8
press, 34–5
prisoners, 10–11, 19–20, 22, 25
Prisoners and Dependants
    Association, 9–10
proportional representation, 64
Provisional Government, 53–4,
    63
    Collins's role, 85–8
    Civil War, 89–96

Republican Land Bank, 47
Rooney, William, 38–9, 108
Roscommon, County, 56
Royal Irish Constabulary (RIC),
    16, 22, 24, 29, 43
Russia, 15

Sinn Féin, 10, 12–14, 22, 48–9,
    51, 112. see also Dáil Éireann
    foundation of, 38–9
    elections, 55–60
    Treaty talks, 67, 75–7
Sligo, County, 26
Smith, Sgt, 29
Smuts, Jan, 112
social policy, 102–3
Soloheadbeg, Co. Tipperary, 16
'Squad', 20–21
Stack, Austin, 10–17
Statute of Westminster 1930, 72
Strickland, General, 25

taxation, 103
Tipperary, County, 14, 27
Tobin, Liam, 25
Treacy, Sean, 16
Truce, 1921, 29–31, 66–7
Tyrone, County, 23, 57, 65, 74,
    78

United States of America, 72–3
fund-raising, 41, 44, 45, 46,
48

Volunteers, 108

War of Independence, 34–5, 59,
67, 91, 94
begins, 16–29
assassinations, 20–21, 25–6,
28–9, 43
Dáil Loan, 42–9

escapes, 51–2
water power, 106
Waterford, County, 57
Wexford, County, 7
Wilson, President Woodrow, 16,
40, 59
Wilson, Sir Henry, 64
Wolfe Tone, Theobald, 108
Worthington-Evans, Sir Laming,
53

Young Irelanders, 37–8